THE SPIRITS OF MINDORO

Catherine Davis

Before becoming a freelance writer, Catherine Davis spent twenty years in book publishing, the last nine years as managing editor and then executive editor at a major Christian publishing house. Her books include *Talking with God, Count Your Blessings, A Place Called Heaven, A Place Called Home, Faithful Friend* (Lifejourney), and *Baby Bible Devotions* (Chariot). Catherine and her husband live in Barrington, Illinois. She has fond memories of attending China Inland Mission prayer meetings at the CIM house outside Chicago while she was a student at Moody Bible Institute.

The Spirits of Mindoro

The true story of how
the gospel came to a strangely-prepared,
demon-fearing people

CATHERINE DAVIS

MONARCH
BOOKS

First published by Monarch Books 1998

ISBN 1 85424 424 8

Editorial Office: Monarch Books,
Broadway House, The Broadway, Crowborough,
East Sussex TN6 1HQ

The author gratefully acknowledges
the valuable resources of the following books:
Barbara Flory Reed, *Beyond the Great Darkness*
(OMF, 1987);
Caroline Stickley, *Broken Snare* (OMF, 1975).

British Library Cataloguing Data
A catalogue record for this book is available
from the British Library.

Designed and produced for the publishers by
Bookprint Creative Services
P.O. Box 827, BN21 3YJ, England
Printed in Great Britain.

CONTENTS

FOREWORD

In 1949 Chairman Mao Tse Tung's Communist Party in China smugly deported several hundred OMF missionaries from the world's most populous nation. No doubt Mao and his party leaders thought they had dealt Christianity a major set-back.

Little did they realise that the churches the missionaries had planted in China were capable of multiplying and thriving without further missionary presence. The number of Christians worshipping in China's churches has increased at least 100 times since 1949.

Little did China's communists realise something else. Their mass deportation of missionaries from China was in reality a mass exportation of spiritual blessing from China to other nations across Southeast Asia. Indonesia, Singapore, Malaysia, Thailand, and, yes, the Philippines were recipients of that export.

And that is the setting for Catherine Davis' remarkable story *The Spirits of Mindoro*. It is another awesome account of gospel precursors hidden and waiting to open the gates of a culture for Jesus.

Don Richardson

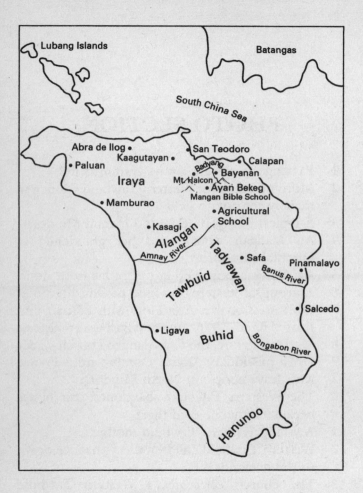

Mindoro Island

PHOTO SECTION

CAST OF MAIN CHARACTERS

(in order of appearance)

Hazel Page

Canadian who joined the first missionaries to the Mangyan on Mindoro Island after being forced to leave China. Because of her language expertise, she worked with at least three of the six Mangyan tribes.

Dr Jim Broomhall

Englishman and nephew of Hudson Taylor who was sent to Mindoro after leaving China. First superintendent of Mindoro work.

Marie Barham

Another missionary from the China exodus, she pioneered the work with the Buhid tribe on Mindoro.

Frances Williamson

From China she went to Mindoro to pioneer the work with the Iraya tribe.

Anghel Anias

The first Mangyan believer, and a leader in the Iraya tribal church.

Russell and Barbara Reed

American couple whose determination and love for the simple life prepared them for discouragement in reaching the elusive Tawbuid tribe.

Bob and Joy Hanselman

American ex-serviceman and his Australian wife who took over the work with the Buhid tribe when Marie Barham left.

Caroline Stickley

Secretary from Philadelphia who was one of the first missionaries to contact the Tadyawan tribe.

David and Beverley Fuller

They met and married on Mindoro, then were active in launching the Mangyan Bible School.

Grandma 'Flower'

One of the first Mangyan believers, she regularly left her village of Bayanan to share her faith with others up and down the slopes of Mount Halcon.

Palay

Alangan who, ever since his conversion as a teenager, was tireless in his efforts to evangelise his people.

Morven Cree Brown

New Zealander who worked with Hazel Page and Beverley Erickson in Alangan territory.

Ann Flory

Sister of Barbara Reed whose work focused on the children of the Mangyan.

Dode Pack

Caroline Stickley's partner in the work among the Tadyawan.

Pedro

The cross-eyed, wild-haired Mangyan who was one of the first Tadyawan believers.

Mariano Lakoy

Mangyan leader of the Alangan tribal church.

Carding Bulaklak

Mangyan leader of the Iraya tribal church.

INTRODUCTION

China, 1951

She stood by the truck with her arms raised, tall and calm, ignoring the fly that buzzed near her sweating face. The summer breeze blew her skirt against her long legs properly covered by cotton stockings. A twist of thick brown hair fell from the tight topknot at the back of her head.

It was like every other check-point. Uniformed men ordered all sixteen of them to get out of the back of the truck and lay their baggage and bedding out on the ground. But this time they were told, 'Keep your hands up, all of you, or be shot!'

She knew they meant it. The communists were not playing games. So far, not one of the more than six hundred China Inland Mission members had been killed, but there had been threats, and their presence posed a danger to the growing groups of faithful Chinese Christians. The order had finally come through from the mission's Shanghai head-quarters: leave as soon as you can. From all over China, missionaries were saying tearful farewells and travelling by foot, by boat, by train, by truck to Canton and then over the bridge to freedom in Hong Kong.

Thank goodness the fly had gone to pester one of the others. She could feel the muscles in her shoulders tighten. Her arms felt bloodless and weak. 'Try not to think about it. This will soon be over, and then we'll be on our way again. Maybe we can invent a new game to pass the time. Thank you, Lord, for keeping our spirits up.'

She remembered one of those last days in Paoshan. She could hear the guns at the execution grounds off the path that led by the mission com-pound. Then stern voices and trudging footsteps sent her running to the ladder leaning against the inside compound wall. She climbed up just in time to see one of their Chinese Christian friends being marched down the path in chains. In a few minutes he would be shot, and she could do nothing. She wanted to call out to him, 'Goodbye! We'll see you in heaven.' But she couldn't.

'Hazel,' a voice hissed next to her. 'It's your turn.' With his gun, the official motioned for her to open her baggage. At least now she could put her arms down.

CHAPTER ONE

During the early days of 1951 the China Inland Mission made the painful decision to pull its missionaries out of China. The decision was made primarily for the safety of Chinese Christians whose lives were in danger because of their faith and their association with the 'foreign aggressors'. Communist officials dangled exit visas before missionary noses, but often waited months before signing them. Even then, for no apparent reason, travel plans were delayed and CIM men and women, reluctant to leave but knowing they must, were left in a limbo of uncertainty.

The orders to leave were especially difficult for missionaries like Hazel Page, who had sensed a pull toward China since her childhood in British Columbia. At five years old, Hazel answered the question, 'And what will you be when you grow up?' with, 'I'm going to be a missionary to China.'

Hazel kept this goal before her, even rejecting an

offer from her high school French teacher who recognised this serious young student's linguistic skills and wanted to pay her way to France to study the language. Hazel thanked her, saying, 'I'm sorry, I can't go to France. I've told the Lord I'm going to China.'

After high school graduation Hazel's parents needed her at home while her two older sisters took jobs to help with family finances. Her neighbourhood became her mission field, and she spent many afternoons holding children's meetings and in house-to-house visitation. One night a CIM missionary from China spoke at her church's Young People's Meeting, detailing the excuses she had given God for not leaving home in answer to her clear 'call'. Every one of those excuses sounded familiar to Hazel.

She went home from the meeting and told her mother, 'I know the Lord is speaking to me about going to China, but I also know that you need me here at home.'

'Actually,' her mother said, 'with all your activities you're seldom home anyway. You might as well go to China if that's what God is saying to you.'

At Saskatoon Bible College where she enrolled, Hazel broke off a relationship with a young man bound for a mission field in South America. 'I told the Lord I will go to China, and I must do that.'

But the bombing of Pearl Harbour cancelled visas into China and Hazel spent the next five years after graduation teaching at the Bible college and then in tribal language translation in Mexico. When CIM notified her in 1946 that China visas were again available, Hazel went joyfully on her way, and arrived at the mission headquarters in Shanghai just in time for the New Year's Eve communion service.

Hazel wanted to get through language school as quickly as possible to start translating a tribal Chinese dialect. Her gift with languages was tailor-made for her passion: that all people should be able to read the Bible in their own tongue. But before she could finish studying in Kunming and go to her assignment with the Shan tribe near the Thai border, the mission asked her to go to Chungking to assist the large group of newly-arrived missionaries in their introduction to Chinese.

While she worked in Chungking, word came that the communists were advancing quickly to the area. Hazel joined the other missionaries in prayer as they waited in the group of bungalows perched on a hill above the city. With the sound of gunfire in the distance, she committed the situation to the Lord. 'OK, I'm ready to stay here or ready to go before the situation gets worse. It's your choice, Lord.' That night a telegram came saying that the *St Paul*, the same Lutheran-owned plane that had brought in the recruits, would fly in the next morning and Hazel should be on it when it flew back out.

The next day, when the little plane lifted off the runway, Hazel looked out to see the green hills fading into blue mist, and bursts of fire from the ground as communist soldiers ran out onto the runway and futilely shot at the plane.

Hazel arrived back in Kunming in time for the shelling of that city by the communists. Then, under military escort, she returned to Paoshan. The missionaries, safe for now in the compound with its secure fence and big house, didn't want to leave. But when the word came that all China missionaries were being evacuated, they knew they must go. They spent the next weeks planning carefully, packing only the amount of baggage allowed them by the communist officials, hiding cherished items for the time they would return. Hazel found a safe place under the front steps of the house for her 'Handy Andy', an all-purpose tool with an axe, hammer, wrench, screwdriver and pliers in one cleverly constructed piece. She would retrieve it when they were allowed to return.

When the communists finally permitted the missionaries to leave, they were ready. They piled into the back of the truck and drove away from the compound, wondering what would happen to the Chinese believers who must stay and face the invaders. And what had God planned for these expatriates who had committed their lives to reaching the Chinese with the good news?

The questions were with them at every checkpoint of the long journey out of China. And they were still there when the truck drove over the bridge from Canton into Hong Kong and pulled up in front of the row of Quonset huts that were temporary quarters for the large group of missionaries coming out of China.

As Hazel waited for passage on a ship out of Hong Kong to England and then home to British Columbia, she prayed that God would show her the next step. 'What does all this mean? I thought you were calling me to China. What do you have in mind, Lord?'

Liangshan, China, 1951

The little group of Nosu Christians still waited beside the river, black capes falling back from brave shoulders as they raised their arms to wave, now and then brushing a hand across a cheek wet with tears. The trail, crowded with mules carrying packs and people, climbed from the river up into the wild-looking hills. Dr A.J. 'Jim' Broomhall twisted around on his mule, Belinda, to get one last look at these brothers and sisters—the reason he had come to China back in 1938. The Great Cold Mountains they called this remote land of more than one million Nosu tribespeople. For Jim Broomhall, coming to China as a CIM missionary was coming home. He was a nephew of Hudson Taylor, the revered founder of the China Inland Mission, and had been born in China of missionary parents. A degree from medical school in London readied him to answer his call to the Nosu tribe. But because of the Japanese invasion, four years passed before he and his bride could leave the coastal areas of China for the inner regions of the Nosu.

Jim gave Belinda an affectionate pat. She had carried him along the river banks of this beautiful but bleak country as he treated patients who had never before known a doctor's care. He had bent his six-foot-plus body to walk under the low doorposts of house after house, inviting them to the clinic where he and two nurses performed miracles. At least that's what it seemed to the people. A sixteen-year-old could now walk after two intricate operations at the primitive facilities. A leper, who before would have been beaten to death, was cured. But more important, hundreds of Nosu whom Satan held in fearful captivity now had new life and hope through Jesus Christ.

Up ahead, Broomhall could see two of his young daughters bouncing along in huge baskets hung on either side of a large mule. Sturdy tribesmen carried the other two–still babies, really–in baskets on their backs. The two nurses and his petite wife, Janet, her soft brown hair covered by a warm hat, rode near them. How long would it take to reach the Yangtze? And how long then to the border and the safety of Hong Kong? Would the rumour materialise–that the communists planned to ambush them at a mountain pass, kill the adults and carry off the children?

Jim's heart lightened as he took a deep breath of the crisp mountain air. God's plan was still in place. And if the plan included their reaching Hong Kong safely, the only remaining question was the next step. Did God have other work for them—perhaps to take the light to a similar stronghold of the evil one where their experience with the Nosu tribe could be an advantage?

Four months later, the Broomhall party passed through the barbed wire at the Hong Kong border, ready for the next step in God's plan.

Kolorama, Australia, 1951

An atmosphere of expectancy charged the room as, one after another, the six men prayed. With more than four hundred of their people still waiting to leave China—until now the total focus of the China Inland Mission—the directors of the mission gathered for a critical conference. Each man was conscious of the big question-mark on the future of the China Inland Mission. Could this be the end of the work begun by Hudson Taylor almost a hundred years ago? Or was this the beginning of the mission's expansion into new territory—an opportunity to reach places their founder could hear calling him from beyond China's borders? If they disbanded, what about the thousands of faithful supporters whose prayers and gifts had sustained them; what about the areas of the world still with no witness for Christ? But if they continued, where should they go? Should they concentrate on the millions of Chinese living in other parts of South-east Asia, or should they approach other groups of people in that region who had still not heard the gospel?

The men reminded each other that they had only been the scaffolding of God's building in China. The building would remain even though they were removed. But the question remained. Did God want the scaffolding set up in another place, and if so, where?

Some of them recalled Hudson Taylor's response when he first sighted the islands in the archipelago between the Indian and Pacific Oceans on his way to China in 1853. The double-masted sailing ship, *The Dumfries*, had carried him all the way from Liverpool and around the Cape of Good Hope. As the ship neared the north-eastern coast of Australia, the beautiful, fertile islands came into view: Indonesia, Guinea, Borneo, Malaysia, and then the Philippines. Taylor wrote, 'Oh what work for the missionary! Island after island, many of them unknown, some densely peopled, but no light, no Jesus, no hope full of bliss! My heart yearns over them. Can it be that Christian men and women will stay comfortably at home and leave these souls to perish?'

For two days the mission directors had prayed. Now, on the third day of the conference they were ready to make a decision. As the last prayer was raised and the discussion points reviewed, the Holy Spirit united them in a decision: the China Inland Mission would continue, and its next steps would be taken in the countries of South-east Asia. Further, teams would be sent out to assess the needs of other groups of unevangelised people throughout the area.

Two China veterans, Ray Frame and Steve

Knights, were asked to check out the Philippine Islands, particularly the unevangelised tribes living in that sprawl of seven thousand large and small bits of land in the South Pacific. Seven hundred of these islands were large enough to be inhabited. Many of these held tribal groups with unwritten languages.

The men spent two months travelling the islands on crowded, dusty buses, on creaky ferries and home-made canoes, by horse-drawn cart and on foot. Weary and footsore, but encouraged by the possibilities, they returned to CIM's temporary headquarters in Hong Kong to write their report. In view of the large Chinese-speaking population of the islands, they recommended that experienced ex-China missionaries be sent to assist the work of other missions with the Chinese already in progress. 'Beyond that,' they wrote, 'We see no reason why an attempt should not be made very soon among the Mangyan tribes of Mindoro Island.'

When they hiked into the jungle areas and up through mountain passes on Mindoro, eighty-five miles south of Manila, the men had been touched by the plight of the six primitive tribes living in the mountains that run up and down the centre of the island. Ray Frame wrote later that 'Steve Knights could not get them off his mind'. The tribal people, known as Mangyan, were animist. They believed that malicious spirits lived in the rocks and trees, mostly bent on their destruction. They seldom or never ventured out from the dense forest areas and interior valleys where they had retreated years before to escape the exploitation of everyone from the early Spanish conquerors to some present-day lowlanders. They were peace-loving people living in material and spiritual poverty and fear, existing primarily through their expert knowledge of the jungle.

Even an anthropologist who had lived and worked among the Mangyan could not give much information about them. The problem was finding them. Some did live on the fringes of the lowlands, acting as sentries, watching for unwelcome visitors, but many more–perhaps thousands–were believed to be hidden in the valleys and up in the ridges of the mountains, leaving their crops and shelters and moving on whenever civilisation came too close. No one knew just how many Mangyan there were, but the anthropologist estimated at least fifteen thousand–a number that would prove to be less than a third of the actual Mangyan population.

Apparently, the Mangyan were first to inhabit Mindoro, followed by a few venturesome Filipinos who settled in the coastal areas. Around 1225, Chinese traders travelled to the island because, though small (only about sixty miles wide and one hundred miles long) they considered the island an important trading centre. It was not that far for their ships, laden with porcelain, silk and tea, to come to the wealthy settlement of Mamburao on Mindoro's west coast from China's southern ports. After unloading their goods, the ships would leave with beeswax, pearls, sandalwood and tortoiseshell.

In 1570 Spaniards destroyed Mamburao and

sailed north to capture Manila and make it the centre of their new Philippine colony. The Mangyan chose to ignore the silk traders and sword-carrying conquerors and simply retreated further back into the hills and crevices of the mountains. Even when America defeated Spain in Manila Bay in 1898 and annexed the Philippine Islands, opening the way for Protestant missionaries, the Mangyan were not affected. They continued to let the rest of the world go by, planting their sweet potatoes, eating their bananas, and trying to appease the spirits who constantly kept them off balance.

After the brief occupation by the Japanese in the 1940s, the Philippines became a republic and the economy began to grow. The population of Mindoro increased as did the demand for the natural resources of the island, making the conflict between the Mangyan and the lowlanders more intense. The peace-loving Mangyan were no match for land-hungry immigrants.

Almost two years before Frame and Knights surveyed Mindoro, two women from Gospel Recordings in California heard a lecture by the anthropologist who had studied the Mangyan tribes. Gospel Recordings specialised in recording Scripture passages in uncommon languages. The women realised that here were at least six more opportunities to communicate the gospel through recorded word. They made arrangements to spend four weeks on Mindoro, and with the help of Filipinos who knew Mangyan in the fringe areas, they recorded significant Bible verses in several of the Mangyan tribal languages.

At the same time Marie Barham, a CIM missionary in Chekiang, China, felt an unexplainable yearning to evangelise unreached tribal people. After Marie was forced to leave China along with hundreds of other missionaries in 1951, mission officials began lining up workers for the new areas. Mindoro had been chosen as one of the South-east Asia locations to be evangelised. 'How would you like to work among unreached tribes in the Philippines?' the officials asked Marie.

While Marie pondered and prayed over her next move, she met the two women from Gospel Recordings and heard a firsthand account of their trip to Mindoro. The women described the fear and poverty and enslavement to demon spirits of the few Mangyan they had met. This encounter sealed Marie's decision, and she wrote, 'Assuredly . . . the Lord has called me to preach the gospel to the Mangyans!'

Marie arrived in Manila in April 1952, a year after leaving China, and was welcomed by two missionary couples who had come earlier to set up a base of operations and begin working in the city. She discovered that her partner in the Mindoro venture would be another China veteran, Frances Williamson, who had been in Anhwei, north-west of the Chekiang region where Marie worked. Frances had been a teacher in rural Minnesota schools before she enrolled in the Bible missionary course at Moody

Bible Institute in Chicago. She had wanted to be a missionary since she was eleven years old. Since January when she arrived in Manila, Frances had been studying Tagalog, the trade language of the Philippines.

Only a few days after Marie arrived, she and Frances boarded a pre-dawn bus for the southern coast to catch a ferry to Mindoro. Marie's short, stocky frame seemed larger than actual next to the tiny Frances. In their modest dresses and grey-streaked brown hair pinned up in practical topknots, neither woman looked ready to meet a primitive jungle tribe. Being well into mid-life, either of them could have requested a less exacting assignment than the one facing them.

Besides the necessary supplies and equipment, their trunks held a wind-up phonograph and gospel records in Mangyan languages.

CHAPTER TWO

Mindoro, the Philippines

As long as I can remember I have lived up here in this forest of lush green fern and banana palm. When I climb the trail to the top of the mountain I can see to the end of the world—the sea way off in the blue-grey distance, the tall coconut palms dotting the landscape near the lowland villages, and the river, always the river, snaking in and out of the flat lands down below.

It's safe up here. Safe from lowlanders who force us to work in the mahogany forests for little or no pay, and beat us if we refuse. They treat us like animals. Some of them even believe that we Mangyan have tails! When we hear these people coming we disappear deep into the forest. No wonder the great great grandfathers left the lowlands to live up here in the jungle-covered hills. It's safe.

But it's not safe from the spirits. They watch us and listen to our conversations. Yesterday I saw one—a small dark shadow creeping along behind me on the steep mountain path. I knew he would make me fall if I weren't careful. I can still feel my heart bumping in my chest as I hid in the bushes until he left. I should have known there would be trouble when I heard the call of the koykolo bird in the morning.

Sometimes I sit by my fire pit and think about the prophecy. The Old One says that long ago one of the grandfathers met a beautiful shining spirit down by the stream. This was surely a good spirit. 'After you die,' the spirit said, 'people will come from another land. They will be white people—teachers, and they will know your language. You must tell your people to listen to what they say and obey their teaching.'

I wonder if these teachers will come before I die? Perhaps so. After all, I'm a young man.

San Teodoro, Mindoro, the Philippines, 1952

Frances Williamson watched the rain shower the window with huge drops that slithered down the pane, obliterating the view of the white caps that disturbed the face of the South China Sea. It had been raining for two days, and even if it stopped by morning the road to the Mangyan village would be nothing but mud. She'd have to be patient and wait. She drew a handkerchief from her pocket and wiped her forehead for the sixteenth time. With the humidity this high, the rain made little difference.

It had been six months since she and Marie Barham moved here to San Teodoro to try to reach the 'Iraya' tribe of Mangyan. Friendly Filipinos let them this seaside house, and were helping them to learn Tagalog.

'Lord, thank you again for guiding us here,' she prayed out loud. This appeared to be a perfect place to begin the new work. The Mangyan in this area spoke Tagalog, and were less afraid of lowlanders than the ones further up in the mountains. In fact, after several visits to Kaagutayan, the closest Mangyan village, they had formed a friendship with the headman, Anghel Anias. Now he supervised the building of a house for Frances so she could live in his village during the week. She'd have to keep her house here in San Teodoro for weekends so she could buy supplies and pick up her mail.

It shouldn't take long to build a Mangyan house. She could be sure of a bamboo platform raised about five feet off the ground, and a Nipa-palm-thatched roof. But walls? Maybe one or two. She hoped they'd remember to build some kind of steps. That single pole leaning against the house wasn't the easiest way to climb up, even though the Mangyan made it look simple. They were so nimble and graceful. And she hoped the Mangyan wouldn't think she was putting on airs when she brought in a table and stools and a camp-bed. Now that she was approaching fifty, sleeping on a straw mat, as the Mangyan did, meant backache in the morning.

On days like this she missed Marie who had moved to Salcedo, a hundred miles south, to try to make contact with another Mangyan tribe, the

Buhid. Frances felt a thrill of excitement thinking about the thousands of Mangyan living in remote mountain areas up and down Mindoro. Would they find them all? They must! Here were people in captivity to an abusive spirit worship that resulted in the death of newborn babies, the sacrificing of animals much needed for food, the sacrifice of a year's crops for the whim of a vindictive shaman. What would it be like to live in fear that every move you made might bring the wrath of beings you could not see? So much fear—even of people, even of other Mangyan tribes.

'We are not afraid of you,' Anghel Anias had told her. 'But the Mangyan who live back in the forest are afraid of people who wear clothes, and especially of people who wear shoes. I will invite these forest people to Kaagutayan to meet you. When they get to know you they will no longer be afraid.'

This was a good start.

England, 1953

Dr Jim Broomhall drained the last drop from his cup of afternoon tea, and began rereading the small stack of Mindoro reports on the table beside him. Since he'd received the reports from CIM headquarters, along with a letter requesting that he take leadership of the Mangyan tribal work in the Philippines, he almost had them memorised.

Ever since he and Janet fled China, they had prayed earnestly for God's direction. What would be the next step? Now that this assignment had been offered, Jim (and Janet too) sensed an inner peace about accepting it. Their experience with the Nosu tribe would not be wasted. But the Mangyan presented challenges they didn't have with the Nosu. What would it take to accomplish the task of bringing the gospel to the Mangyan?

Well, first they would have to find them. According to the reports, many of the fifteen to twenty thousand Mangyan on Mindoro lived in the almost inaccessible interior. Most of the tracks to their villages were sometimes muddy, often perpendicular paths known only to the tribes. But finding the Mangyan was only the beginning. Since the majority understood only their own tribal tongue, they would have to learn those languages before they could communicate the gospel. And there were at least *six* different languages.

Those two women–Frances Williamson and Marie Barham–what courage and determination! Already they had managed to contact a few Mangyan living on the edge of civilisation. They would need more workers–many more, if they were to reach people in each of the tribes.

Then they would face the matter of primitive living conditions. The China Inland Mission followed the policy of its founder. Hudson Taylor believed in becoming one with the people–adapting to their manner of living as much as possible and altering it only as necessary for health and efficiency. Jim had seen the effectiveness of this policy in China.

He knew it would be the backbone of their approach with the Mangyan. But, can we ask families with children to live in a Mangyan village? Some of the reports made clear the stark and unsanitary conditions they could expect.

His hand rubbed his clean-shaven chin thoughtfully. He tried to picture his sweet and petite wife Janet managing life with four young daughters in a grass hut balanced on shaky poles. He scanned the reports to read again the description of the Mangyan's problems with some Filipino immigrants. 'They have threatened to kill us and molest our wives if we do not forsake the jungle land we have cleared with our own hands and leave it to them.' More chilling, however, were the accounts of their daily battles with the spirit world.

Jim had witnessed the power of evil in China. But he had never met a group of people whose lives were orchestrated by demonic spirits. 'This could be the challenge of a lifetime,' he thought. He laid the papers on the table and got up to kneel beside the chair. 'Heavenly Father, through Jesus Christ you have called us to be your servants to people on this distant island who seem to be dominated by your adversary. I thank you, Father, that you are in charge. It is in your strength that we go.'

South China Sea, the Philippines, 1953

Seventeen days on the magnificent ship out of San Francisco to Manila made this wooden ferry seem frail and uncertain, its old timbers slapping against the waves. Hazel Page towered above the diminutive Filipinos beside her as she stood with her arms resting on the waist-high railing, watching the Batangas pier recede slowly from view. She pulled a handkerchief out of her handbag and patted the back of her neck. Then she tried to tuck in the locks of hair that had escaped from the rolls pinned up around the sides and back of her head. In less than three hours she and Frances Williamson would land in Calapan, the busy little capital of eastern Mindoro Island. Then she would at last be on her way to the tribespeople who had occupied her thoughts since she had heard of their need for a translator–the Mangyan of Mindoro. Frances had asked for a good linguist to help her translate the language of one of the Mangyan tribes. She hoped to reach the Iraya who lived back in the forest and spoke only their own language. The China Inland Mission contacted Hazel, knowing of her desire to go to a tribal group. It had taken months to get a work visa for the Philippines–another opportunity to learn patience.

Frances, small and dainty–almost fragile-looking in a flowered print dress with a lace collar–had come all the way up to Manila to meet her and escort her back to Mindoro. When they walked to the ferry Hazel had to stoop to carry on a conversation with her. The little ferry chugged along cheerfully, never seeming to stray very far from land. Hazel relaxed for a while on the rows of wooden seats filled with Filipinos and boxes and bags of all sizes. A cockerel crowed from a wooden cage at the end of the row, and another answered from somewhere near the back of the long enclosed deck. The sea breeze offered some relief from the stifling heat and humidity of Manila. Maybe it would be cooler on Mindoro.

When she joined Frances again at the railing, a green-covered island loomed close by on the right side of the boat. 'That's Verde Island, and there . . . right behind Verde you can see Mindoro!' Frances pointed out, her eyes sparkling with anticipation.

Like a great mother guarding her young, smoky-blue Mindoro rose up behind Verde, dominating the horizon. To the west Hazel could barely make out the slate-grey ghost of a huge mountain on the island, surrounded by clouds. 'That's Mount Halcon,' Frances explained. 'Some say there are thousands of Mangyan living on its slopes and in its valleys.'

The ferry passed through a narrow channel between tiny twin islands with identical white sand beaches, and now Hazel could see what must be Calapan's harbour with its single pier. Above the town, wave after wave of hills built up to hazy mountains in the distance.

Before the ferry docked, people poured out of their seats, clutching their baggage. Hazel and Frances were pushed and shoved down the narrow wooden stairs to the crowded deck below. Outside they found buses and horse-drawn carts waiting for passengers. A bus with one side completely open to the elements dropped them at the hotel in downtown Calapan. The two-storey wooden building was situated off the dirt street not far from the open market that stretched around a corner and up to the bridge over the river. The sweet smell of peanut brittle mixed in with the ever-present smoke of brush fires, but neither aroma could blot out the smell of the fish market. Hazel pushed her glasses up on her nose from where they kept sliding in the heat. She looked out of the hotel window and memorised the scene. Tomorrow she would leave Calapan with Frances and go up the coast to San Teodoro to begin her work with the Mangyan.

CHAPTER THREE

Yesterday three men from the lowlands came to my brother's house hunting for wild pig and deer. 'Show us where to find the wild pig and we will pay you,' they said. My brother didn't want to go with them, but he was afraid of their guns.

'We're hungry,' the men said. 'Before we go you must kill two chickens so we can eat.' My brother had already killed one of his chickens the day before to sacrifice to the demons. His wife's mother was very ill. Maybe the demons would see the sacrifice and make her well.

My brother's wife roasted the chickens over the fire and gave them to the men. They ate both of them— didn't offer my brother a single piece. When they finished they gave him a little coconut shell filled with cooked rice. That's all! As though that little bit of rice was worth two chickens.

My brother then took them further up the mountain where he had seen wild pig. They didn't find a pig, but

they did spot a deer. After they shot the deer they paid
my brother with a few cigarettes. Cigarettes!

Sometimes I think those lowlanders are as sly and
tricky as the spirits.

Indian Ocean, 1952

'There's more silver on this table than we'd use in
three meals at home!' Barbara Reed remarked as
they sat down to another sumptuous meal served
on exquisite china; the sterling tableware gleamed
on the immaculate linen cloth. From the moment
they boarded the Queen Mary in New York harbour
they had been waited on hand and foot, even though
she and Russell and the other CIM missionary candidates were definitely not in the first-class section.
Now, as they continued their voyage on the Cunard
line from London to Singapore, they encountered
the same luxury. 'For a couple of people who prefer
the simple life, this is something else!' she thought.

Barbara watched a woman in an elegant white
dress walk past the table and let her mind wander
back to their beautiful, simple wedding four years
ago. Wild roses entwined around wispy green fern at
the front railing of the church. The polished wood of
the pews seemed more glowing and golden than
usual. And there was Russell–waiting for her.

Barbara interrupted her reverie to glance at Russell sipping soup from an elegant China bowl. Her
bridegroom–quiet, gentle Russell Reed. Walking
down the church aisle, her eyes had been only on

him. Barbara wore the dress of a generous friend, short and slender like herself, and carried gladiolas from a church member's garden. Her mother had sent money for a veil that fluffed and flowed above her long brown hair. The bridesmaids had been able to borrow identical formal dresses in pastel colours. What a wonder that they exactly fitted each one–even the rather plump one.

Everything had come together so naturally. With Russell just out of national service, and she in her first year at The Bible Institute of Los Angeles, they didn't have a penny. But they had been engaged for over a year. When she made the trip from California to Wisconsin early in the summer, it seemed the right time to be married. Her mother, at home in California, agreed. The University of Wisconsin, where Russell had a place, waived all fees for Barbara–she had excellent entry qualifications and she'd be married to a veteran. With Russell's discharge money they were able to purchase a tiny house trailer, sixteen feet long and six-and-a-half feet wide, with a built-in bed and miniature table, stove and sink. They parked it in the mobile-home park near the university and moved in right after the honeymoon.

Honeymoon. That had been another gift from the Lord. The morning of the wedding they had loaded Russell's parents' big tent into the family car and set it up at the church's empty campsite out beside Lake Wabesa. Some people from the church dropped them off there after the wedding along with enough tinned food to last them for the three days they could take away from their jobs. For these two lovers of adventure and the outdoors, it couldn't have been a more perfect honeymoon.

The two of them shared a commitment to the Lord and to foreign missionary service. Of all the mission fields they'd looked into, China sounded the most interesting and challenging.

After Russell graduated from the University of Wisconsin they had gone west to Oregon. Russell took courses at Multnomah School of the Bible and was then pastor of a small church sponsored by the American Sunday School Union. Barbara got a teaching qualification from a local college and then taught at a Christian secondary school. During this time they had been in constant contact with the China Inland Mission. Then the blow came: CIM planned to pull out of China. They told the mission they would prefer tribal work—anywhere in Southeast Asia and they prayed for God's guidance.

'Wherever it is, I hope the Lord sends us to a tribe way out where no one has ever been,' Barbara had declared.

By autumn she had resigned from her teaching job, Russell had preached his last sermon, and they were off to Philadelphia for CIM candidate school. Then, in late January, they said farewells that would have to last them for four years, and sailed for England.

In England Russell and Barbara and the other Americans joined the British candidates for a few days at Newington Green, the British headquarters of the China Inland Mission. While they were there, the director called each of them into a private meeting and almost reverently handed them a scrap of paper with the actual signature of J. Hudson Taylor. The signatures appeared to be cut from the bottom of letters or from envelopes or documents signed by the founder of the mission. Perhaps this was a way of encouraging the new candidates to identify with the goals of this man who had developed an original, highly effective approach to foreign evangelism.

Barbara felt almost guilty cutting into the juicy roast beef on her plate. It would be a long time before people in England would enjoy food like this. Obviously, they were still suffering the after-effects of World War II. Fuel seemed to be in short supply and rations limited. But the staff at Newington Green managed to keep them adequately fed while they were there. 'Now here we are, all sixteen of us, enjoying an abundance of food on this ship on our way to Singapore–the last stop before our final destination, wherever that will be.'

After the few fast weeks at candidate school in Philadelphia, the scramble to get ready to leave home and family, and the session in England, they welcomed these lazy days of relaxing in the comfortable deck-chairs or playing a leisurely game of shuffleboard in the salty sea air. They were quite aware that all this luxury was in stark contrast to what awaited them in South-east Asia. And they relished the thought. Previously Barbara had dreamt of little palm-roofed huts and cooking over an open fire.

Already they had sailed down the beautiful Mediterranean, through the Suez Canal and around the tip of India. They expected to arrive in Singapore in early March and there study the language and culture of their assigned areas until late autumn. Around the table at meals, during games on the deck, or in the comfortable lounge watching the sun set over the Indian Ocean, Barbara and Russell shared their stories with the other candidates and marvelled at the love and ingenuity of God in bringing them to this place in their lives.

Two of the other Americans in the group were also interested in tribal work. Bob Hanselman, from a small town in New Jersey, told them he was in the armed forces when he committed his life to Jesus Christ. Only two months later, at a missions conference, he knew he was called to be a foreign missionary. Bob could trace the Lord's hand on his life ever since a childhood accident left him seriously burned and doctors thought they'd have to amputate his leg. One of the doctors told his parents, 'He'll die with the operation, anyway. Might as well send him home to die with a crippled leg.' Bob lived, but God had used his handicap to give him a strong feeling for the underdog. Because of the influence of Isobel Kuhn, a CIM missionary supported by Bob's home church, he hoped to work with tribal people who knew what it was to be at the bottom of the pile.

Like Bob, Caroline Stickley was a young adult before she had a conversion experience. After reading the gospels over and over again, she knew that when she committed her life to God she must spend the rest of it in some kind of ministry. Since women didn't seem to be called to the ministry, she would be a missionary to China. She left her job as a secretary in Philadelphia and enrolled at Prairie Bible Institute in Canada. When she was well into her studies, word came from CIM that China had closed. CIM advised her and others who had applied for China service to go to Wycliffe's Summer Institute of Linguistics while the mission geared up for work in South-east Asia. While at SIL, Caroline developed a strong interest in tribal work and hoped to work near the borders of Thailand. Since she had been in Bible school, she'd been praying that God would prepare a group of people somewhere to be ready to receive the message she'd bring to them.

Barbara recalled Caroline's first night out of New York harbour aboard the *Queen Mary*. Caroline grew up terrified of water. At the Bible institute, when missionaries would tell about serving on little islands way off somewhere, she would think, 'I'm so glad God called me to a big country like China where I won't have to be surrounded by water.' While the ship rocked back and forth in the turbulent waters of the Atlantic and the lifeboats banged against the sides, Caroline lay in her bunk, feeling terribly ill. Someone suggested that fresh air would help, so she stumbled up to the deck only to find huge waves rolling the ship so far from side to side that the mast seemed to touch the water. She ran back down to her bunk and decided that if the Lord wanted her to die there on the ocean, it was OK. With that surrender, she told Barbara, her fear left her and had not returned.

Like Caroline, Barbara Reed's faith rested on an assurance that God held her life in his capable hands. It seemed that all of her life up to now had been preparation for what was to come.

Mindoro, the Philippines, 1953

The trip to San Teodoro with Frances presented one new experience after another. The coast route was a feast for the eyes with brilliant green foliage, graceful groves of coconut palm, and now and then a rush of pink or orange as they passed a flowering bush. Hazel thought she had never seen such a turquoise sea. Also, she had never seen ears used as coin holders. While the bus moved down the road, the conductor clung to the poles running up and down the open sides, collecting fares and depositing the coins in his ears. Hazel guessed his pockets were full. Half way there, they had come to a river where the bus drove onto a rickety bamboo raft just large enough for one vehicle. While a man furiously cranked a cable, they travelled to the other side and continued their journey on one of the few roads on the island. The open side of the bus was a mixed blessing. It let in the cool air, and even a refreshing shower when, for a few minutes, it had rained. But for most of the way clouds of dust choked Hazel's throat and sneaked around her glasses into her eyes. Perspiring like this, she supposed she would have brown dribbles running down her face by the time they reached the town.

As they drove into San Teodoro the bus passed a few horse-drawn carts and even a land sledge pulled by a water buffalo. San Teodoro wasn't as large as Calapan, but it did have a post office, a bank, a school, a Roman Catholic church, and a good-sized market. Several small boats in the harbour implied that the main industry here might be fishing.

The bus continued along the beach road. Up ahead a grove of coconut palm leaned towards the ocean as though worshipping the view. Through the trees a house, raised above the ground on four-foot poles and sporting a tall peak on the grass roof, looked bigger than it really was. The bus stopped in front of the house, the driver unloaded Hazel's two trunks and other luggage, and she and Frances climbed up the steps into the place Hazel would now call home.

Tomorrow they would take a trip up to Kaaguta-yan, Frances said, and she could meet the very first Mangyan convert, Anghel Anias. Hazel decided to wear all new clothes for this special trip—a pretty full skirt, white blouse, and white tennis shoes that should be just right for the five-mile walk to the Mangyan village.

The next day they each carried a pack with the supplies they'd need for a few days' stay in the village. Hazel's pack contained matches, sweetened condensed milk, peanut butter, toilet paper, salt, sardines and dried fruit, as well as personal belongings she'd need. She couldn't remember all the contents of Frances' heavy-looking pack, but the older woman certainly didn't appear fragile now as she marched along.

At first the track was just wide enough to be called a decent path. Then, after they came upon a large low area where ten water buffalo were enjoying a sloppy puddle in the heat of the day, the track became two deep muddy ruts with a high dry ridge in the middle. Hazel tried to spare her white shoes and balance on the centre ridge, but soon slipped down into the rut, the mud splashing over her clean new outfit. Her white tennis shoes were now brown tennis shoes. Further up the trail she washed off some of the mud in the river they waded across before they reached the village. It must be close now. They could hear a dog barking and a baby crying. Then the modest group of palm-roofed huts on stilts came into view. A cluster of children played with sticks in the dirt outside one of the huts, their naked little bodies grey with dust. Hazel forgot her muddy clothes and tired muscles. Here were her first Mangyan!

That night, lying on a bed set up on the bamboo

floor of Frances' village house, Hazel couldn't sleep. Something was wrong–a strange heavy feeling. Then she heard the singing. Or was it a chant? She peered out of the cracks in the thatched wall into the blackness where a group of men sat around a fire under one of the nearby houses. This must be what Frances had explained to her–they were 'singing to the spirits', trying to make contact with the spirit world. She shivered. Finally, she asked God to take charge and release her from the heaviness, and fell asleep.

CHAPTER FOUR

It is time for me to have a wife. I know the one I will choose. She's from the village across the river where my cousin lives. He says she is not spoken for, so after the rice is planted I'll go and bring her here.

Why do I want this one? Because she is strong. When I visited my cousin I watched her work. She is not large, but she can dig sweet potatoes faster than anyone, and she can carry five bamboo tubes of water from her headband. Five!

She's a quiet one, but she laughs. I would like a wife who laughs.

I think she'll want to come with me. The second day I was in her village she made herself very clean in the river and even put a flower in her hair. That's a good sign.

The Old One says that until I go and get her I should be very careful. I wouldn't want to make the spirits angry. Especially now.

Calapan, Mindoro, 1953

Jim Broomhall closed his eyes and tried to remember how the icy wind felt when it blew off the Great Cold Mountains of China. Since the first few days in Manila before he and Janet and the girls had come here to Calapan, he had been conscious of the almost adversarial quality of the air—as though it were pressing against you, daring you to breathe or move.

He wiped off the perspiration trickling down his arm and onto the report on the desk. Maybe if he tied the handkerchief around his hand it would blot the moisture before it blurred the ink on the paper. For a few minutes he put the pen down and vigorously fanned himself with his wide black Chinese fan. He glanced around his office seeing the trunk full of books still waiting to be unpacked and the few pieces of furniture already there when they rented this two-storey unpainted wooden house on Ilaya Street in Calapan. 'Ilaya House' they called it. This one should be large enough, at least for now. The three women living on the edges of Iraya and Buhid territories needed a place to come for rest and refreshment. Just the energy needed for daily living in a place without modern conveniences was considerable. Add to that the urgency of learning new languages and customs, and you could soon be in need of a change of scenery.

Street noises filtered in through the open window in front of his desk, along with the dust blown in from another bus driving by on the dirt street. A Filipino woman in a bright flowered dress walked past, balancing her groceries in a bag on her head. Behind her a schoolgirl carried her books in the same way.

What a responsibility he had for these brave women missionaries, now under his supervision as the Philippines Field Superintendent–Marie Barham in Buhid territory and Frances Williamson and Hazel Page with the Iraya. They were tackling a job in a place where some men would refuse to go. They were trying to learn a trade language (as was he) that had no textbooks, and quickly too, for the biggest task still lay ahead: learning the tribal languages so they could reach Mangyan in the back country where the people spoke no Tagalog. As far as they knew, there were at least six Mangyan tribes, each with its own language. They would try to explain the true God to these people, and translate parts of Scripture into their tribal language–the language of the Mangyan heart.

They would need more workers though. Even now the first group of new candidates since the mission had left China, trained in Singapore. At least five of them were designated for Mindoro–one couple, two single women, and a single man. The thought of what this could mean in searching for the tribes in more remote areas sent him to his knees beside the chair.

'Heavenly Father, you have given us a great opportunity to reach these dear people with the extraordinary news of your love and salvation through Christ. Help us to listen carefully for your direction.'

He stayed there on his knees praising God and searching his own heart until Janet called him for the evening meal.

Kaagutayan, Mindoro, 1953

The sweet, almost sickening, smell of Anghel Anias' talcum powder reached Hazel's nose, along with the strong, always-present odour inevitable in a village with no plumbing. Hazel was now familiar with the routine: rise before dawn, see to the 'necessaries' in the privacy of darkness, try to find some time and a place for personal Bible reading and prayer, go to the stream for fresh water that had to be boiled before drinking, cook some rice and coffee for breakfast, and then carry the files full of notes on Mangyan words and phrases, *Young's Concordance*, and several versions of the Bible out to the little porch for their language session. Anghel sat on a floor mat while she and Frances perched on stools. He always came dressed in his best clothes, his black hair with the soft curls characteristic of the Iraya tribe, neatly combed. For three hours each morning Anghel answered their questions about new words and phrases in his native tongue, and helped them translate the gospel of Mark into Iraya. He often told them stories and talked about everyday things. They couldn't have found a better language helper. Anghel not only spoke the Philippine trade language, Tagalog, fluently, but because he had been educated in the government schools, he could speak some English.

In the evenings Anghel and his wife, Rosario, usually came back to the house, bringing a few others from the village. By the light of a kerosene lamp, Hazel and Frances taught them hymns and choruses in Tagalog and helped them memorise a few verses of Scripture.

Hazel watched Anghel's face. Perhaps he finally understood the meaning of a section of Mark they were struggling to translate. Did he really understand enough to be a true believer? They knew he was still consulting the spirits, but he said he believed in Jesus. And what a story he had about the dream thirteen years ago when God revealed his sin to him and told him of his need for forgiveness. He had waited all these years to be forgiven! Could it be that God had prepared this man over a dozen years ago to hear the Christian message through their lips?

Salcedo, Mindoro, 1953

One hundred miles south of San Teodoro, on the eastern coast of Mindoro, Marie Barham's short, sturdy legs were developing good walking muscles. She still had no place to stay in the Buhid villages she visited from her lowland base. After walking sometimes five miles through scratchy cogon grass and rice fields and wading across waist-deep rivers, usually with only the company of her dog, she had time for just two or three hours' study with her Mangyan language helpers before starting the long hike back home.

Marie enlisted Lisigan, an important Buhid chief, to be her language consultant. The Reverend Cruz, the Filipino pastor who befriended her, accompanied her to Lisigan's village the first time they met. While they waited for the chief to appear, the Reverend Cruz said, 'Take off your eyeglasses and shoes so the chief will be less afraid of you.' Lisigan appeared at the edge of the village clearing wearing the typical Buhid costume: thick strands of small red and white beads around his neck, and a loincloth. His small, slender body with the dusty, clay-coloured skin of the Mangyan had seen over fifty years, but he looked no older than forty. Lisigan listened without comment to the gospel records Marie played on the portable phonograph she'd lugged in, then announced that he was ready to tell them some Buhid words. Since that time he had become a valuable language teacher. She hoped he would soon be one of the first Buhid believers.

Today Marie was again house bound because of heavy rain in the mountains. She looked out of the open window. 'It's a good thing I sharpened the sickle earlier in the week,' she thought. 'The grass around the hut will be knee high in no time after all this rain—just the way the snakes prefer it.' She doused herself with a fresh layer of mosquito repellent on her exposed skin, and winced when the lotion stung the fresh bites she'd scratched without thinking. These mosquitoes down here seemed more insistent than the ones in San Teodoro. Then she took out a pad of lined paper, her pen and ink, and began a letter to Hazel.

'Dear Hazel,

Thanks so much for your letter. Yes, I shall be glad for you to come as soon as you can, though really, we have to wait on the weather once you get here. I've been waiting all this week, and thought, after two fine hot days, tomorrow would be the day to go to the village. But Pastor Cruz says the roads would be hopeless . . .

I wouldn't mind walking in all sorts of mud three miles or even six miles more if I had a place to stay overnight and to change clothes when I got there . . . Please don't think I'm downhearted. The weather is in the Lord's hands, and He can give us some fine days even at this season . . .

As I said before, I hope you're bringing mosquito net and pillow.

In Calapan would you kindly get:
2 kilo potatoes
1 or 2 papaya (one fairly green)
2 or 3 green avocados
2 cucumbers
tomatoes, if they are any good
2 smallish cabbages
2 pumelos, if any good
$\frac{1}{2}$ kilo, either beef or pork
string beans, for one meal.
My, that's a list and a half, isn't it? No canned things,

56

they give me real basic prices for them where I get my bread. No more for now. Looking forward to seeing you.

Much love,
Marie.

It was probably best that the three women missionaries didn't see the report written a few months later by a dignitary from the mission headquarters in Singapore after he visited Marie's area.

Although we were able to ride on a lumber truck part of the way from San Teodoro to Salcedo and had a longer lift on the way out, I was about done before the day was over. Most of the trek was over trails which would have been hard to find without a guide. Much of the way was through the jungle–steaming hot jungle. I had felt before that this is a man's job, and this visit has confirmed that opinion!

CHAPTER FIVE

Yes, I do now have a wife. The one I chose from the village across the river was happy to come here with me, and her parents approved. The spirits must have approved also, because all the signs have been good.

The night before I took her home with me nobody in the house heard any spirit voices. Sometimes the spirits will send a dream to warn people not to marry. But this didn't happen. Best of all, there were no ashes under the house the next morning. That's a very good sign.

The house is big enough for all of us. Here in this tribe we continue to live in the family house when we marry. This is good because my mother is getting very old . . . almost forty dry seasons. So she is very glad to have more help. And my wife is strong . . . just like I thought.

Salcedo, Mindoro, 1953

Hazel blew her nose for what she hoped would be the last time for this particular head cold, and followed Marie Barham back down the steep track. They had made three trips since she arrived for a visit with Marie a week ago. The first had been to a Buhid home on the other side of the swollen Bongabon River, still recovering from the August typhoon. A bus took them the first nine miles to the river where they waded across in waist-deep water (probably the reason she'd caught this cold), successfully negotiating the swift current. A mountain stream could quickly sweep you off your feet.

On the other side of the river a friendly Tagalog family gave them lunch while they dried off, and then sent a couple of their daughters with them as guides to the Buhid home. They found the family napping when they arrived, but the people graciously welcomed them and even invited others who lived further up the wet, slippery paths to come and listen to the gospel recordings. The Buhid men, with their red beads and loin cloths, wore their long hair knotted, while the women let theirs hang loose. Besides many strands of the red beads, the women wore a tightly wrapped narrow cloth as a skirt and a small strip of cloth as a kind of bra. A man with long, loose hair, visiting from another tribe, startled Hazel when he grabbed their phonograph and bit each of its four corners. He grabbed a record and bit it the same way. Their guides explained that this was the way he expressed his desire to quickly understand the message!

Hazel heard the reassuring slap of Pastor Cruz's feet on the path behind her. Since Marie's first trip to Salcedo, he had been the one to help her find ways to reach the Buhid. He also provided a house for Marie next door to his family. Today the three of them had ridden in a truck several miles down the middle of the swirling river to a place where steep cliffs rose up from the water. A man there helped them find a well-hidden path up the cliffs to the home of a Mangyan family living high on a plateau. Only an old man and two children were there. When they heard the recordings they evidently couldn't understand them. How would they ever reach the Mangyan when there were all these differences in language and dialect?

Hazel looked down at her stockings spotted with mud and splotches of blood where leeches had found a target. Of all the creatures they met on the tracks, leeches were probably the most irritating, even worse than the large red antican ants with their stinging bites. Unlike the blobs of dark flesh she had seen in Canadian lakes, these were tiny threads, less than an inch long, with a suction cup at one end and a tail like a needle that attacked the skin, injecting a substance that kept the blood from coagulating. As they fed on their victim's blood, they could expand to the size of a large peanut. The muddy mountain trails were full of them, and in the higher areas you could find a green and yellow-striped variety that preferred the victim's eyes. When the three of them reached the river, they would have to stop and remove them from their ankles and legs. The best way, she'd discovered, was with a bamboo stick, pared to a slim blade-like end that you could slide under the leeches, slicing them off the skin. She wished she had remembered to bring a cake of soap with her today. You could foil the determined little pests by soaping your stockings and even the tops of your canvas shoes.

The trail wound down into view of the river, and the trio braced themselves for another encounter with the strong current before they got back to the place where the bus waited to take them home.

Singapore, 1953

For Barbara and Russell Reed and the other Westerners assembled for their first week at the CIM language school, Singapore was an eye-gate to the East. The city was on its way to becoming a modern business centre, but most of these budding missionaries were not ready for the still obvious poverty, the open gutters running with sewage, the people sleeping in the streets.

They ate, slept, and studied language in a large, attractive concrete building overlooking the harbour. The Reeds and the single men occupied the down-stairs bedrooms off the huge dining room. The other married couple and single girls were upstairs.

Everybody helped with daily chores, including washing dishes outside under a covered patio.

Wisely, mission directors set aside the first few days in Singapore for individual discussions about field assignments. Final decisions could then be made, and candidates' minds free to focus on preparation and studying the language of the country to which they were assigned.

Some of the candidates had already asked to be sent to certain areas and were given confirmation at this time unless the committee saw problems with the request. Bob Hanselman, the ex-serviceman from New Jersey, told Russell that he saw his call to downtrodden tribes confirmed when the leaders assigned him to the Mangyan of Mindoro in the Philippines. But the officials rejected Russell and Barbara Reed's request to work among the isolated tribes of north Thailand. Instead, they asked that the Reeds, too, consider the tribes of Mindoro. Barbara and Russell had hoped for a place less civilised, but they believed that God's will could be revealed through those in charge, so they accepted the decision in that spirit.

It seemed that God also had other plans for Caroline Stickley, the secretary from Philadelphia who had conquered her fear of water. Barbara could feel Caroline's disappointment when the directors told her they now believed 'that tribal work in northern Thailand was too dangerous for single women. Rather, they asked Caroline to pray about going to the Philippine island of Mindoro.

The other candidate asked to consider Mindoro, Joy Hayman from Australia, seemed the most equipped for the assignment. Barbara loved to hear Joy's stories of being an 'MK' (missionary's kid) in China. She had lived there while her parents served with the CIM, and even survived the hijacking by pirates of a ship carrying missionaries' children home from boarding school. Like many of the others, Joy wanted to be a missionary to China. When the doors closed the mission advised her to attend linguistics school in Melbourne, where her interest in tribal work began. She had come to Singapore ready to offer herself as a tribal worker who could do language translation.

While Russell and Barbara and the other candidates prepared for their first assignments with CIM, the directors continued the reorganisation of the mission and signed documents officially changing the name from China Inland Mission to Overseas Missionary Fellowship. As OMF, the mission attained status in the Philippines as an official corporation and could apply for visas under its own name. Even so, it took several months for visas to come through for the five people in Singapore bound for the Philippines. When they did it was November, close to the time the group planned to sail for Manila.

The Reed's anticipation of their Mindoro assignment was now matched by anticipation of the approaching birth of their first child, due on 1 December. Just after their Philippine visas came through, a message came from OMF's Manila office saying, 'Get the Reeds to Manila as soon as you can. If that baby is born outside the Philippines it will need a visa, and that could take another nine months!'

Only a PanAm prop plane flew from Singapore to Manila. Barbara, eight and a half months pregnant, climbed on the plane with Russell, eager to be off to the place and people that now called to their hearts. After a half-hour stop in Saigon where civil war kept them on the plane while workers sprayed it with mosquito repellent, the couple arrived in Manila. Eleven days later their first son was born. Less than three weeks later, they were ready to leave for Mindoro.

At the Manila airport, Russell kissed her goodbye, and Barbara climbed up the metal stairway and through the door of the old DC3, carrying her seventeen-day-old son, Ricky, secure in his new blanket. The others, Russell, Caroline Stickley, Bob Hanselman and Joy Hayman, would take the ferry from Batangas. She would arrive first, landing at Calapan's diminutive airport just behind the hills of the city.

Barbara settled into one of the seats and let her mind wander. For months now she had tried to picture in her mind what Mindoro would be like. She imagined living in a remote area surrounded by jungle where she and Russell would have to plan carefully for survival, especially with a young child. Who would Ricky play with? It could get lonely for a little boy in an isolated area. It could get lonely for adults too. Barbara knew how much she enjoyed people contact. Of course there would be people–when they found them. The reports from Marie Barham showed how difficult it could be to make contact with the Mangyan. And she knew that some tribes had not even been found yet. She shifted the baby into a more comfortable position. 'I wonder how long it will take to finish Tagalog study?' she thought. She and Russell were eager to get on with the real reason they had come here: to tell the Mangyan about God's love through Christ. She felt the plane dip to one side and change direction. Outside the window shadowy mountains were very close and she could see a dark ribbon running between the hills near the sea. That must be the airport.

When they landed in Calapan, a December rain pelted the plane as it taxied down the too-short runway. Almost before it rolled to a stop, Barbara had wrapped the blanket around baby Rick and made her way to the door. When it opened she could see a tall, smiling gentleman carrying a huge black umbrella waiting below. He introduced himself as Dr Jim Broomhall, and guided her carefully to their transportation–a small horse-drawn carriage with two big wheels and one seat for passengers behind the driver. This was a *kalesa*, Dr Broomhall explained. Barbara was grateful the kalesa had a small canvas roof and plastic covering the sides as they bumped along the muddy road to the mission home. Suddenly the carriage lurched and stopped, rocking uncertainly. Dr Broomhall steadied Barbara with the baby in her arms while the driver got out and replaced the rubber rim on one of the wheels. Nothing serious. The driver signalled for the horse to go forward, and they were on their way again. Barbara looked out at the banana palms beside the road dripping with rain and bent with the wind, and felt a tingle of excitement. The Mindoro adventure had begun.

Three Hills, Alberta, Canada, 1953

Beverley (Bev) Erickson quickly brushed her blonde hair, adjusted her glasses, and glanced at her image in the mirror. The high cheekbones and wide blue eyes gave away her Swedish heritage. In fact, in her home church in Turlock, California, some services were still conducted in Swedish. She was the only one in her family who attended the church, and it was there that she had first sensed God calling her to Africa as a missionary. But in her last year here at Prairie Bible Institute God seemed to be turning her attention elsewhere.

She picked up an envelope from her desk and checked the stamp. Inside was her carefully written application to the Overseas Missionary Fellowship for work in South-east Asia. She'd heard the rumour that if you sent an application to OMF with the stamp glued on crooked, you'd never be accepted. She dropped the letter in the postbox on her way to class and prayed, 'The next step is up to you, Lord.'

CHAPTER SIX

I will miss the Old One—he was the one who would not let us forget the prophecy. 'The teachers will come,' he would say.

Everyone knew that he had a very powerful personal spirit who would talk to him and sometimes help him. But when he became so ill, the spirit didn't help him. For many days my wife tried to get him to eat some rice or a fresh juicy grub. Every night my brother and I gathered around the fire with the others and sang to the spirits. We hoped they would let the Old One live. We even sacrificed our last pig in exchange for his life. When we were afraid that he might die in the house—if he did, we'd have to burn it down—we carried him out into the forest and laid him on a pile of leaves and built a shelter over him with palm branches. That's where he died.

I buried him far away from the house, near the place where he died. I was afraid because it's true that a dead person's spirit can bite you and make you sick enough to die so you will join him. But I wore my string of animal teeth tied together with a bell to keep the spirits away. It must have worked because I'm feeling strong and well, even after staying in the forest for nine days. That's the way it has to be when you are the one who does the burying.

Today my wife looked sad, and I said, 'Don't be discouraged. The teachers will come.'

She smiled and said, 'You sound just like the Old One.'

Calapan, Mindoro, 1954

With the recently arrived candidates already into the second phase of their language study, Jim Broomhall continued to wrestle with the best way to handle the mammoth task before them all. He believed that the principles Hudson Taylor had used so successfully in China were foundations they could build on here on Mindoro:

1. Their primary reason for being here was to preach Christ, not to westernise the people or even to bring them medical, material or literacy help. They were here to be the scaffolding of God's building and would stay only until the building could stand on its own.

2. Their approach would be to adapt as much as possible to the local manner of life, modifying it only as necessary for health and efficiency.

3. They would respect even the most primitive of these people as intelligent and sensitive individuals,

and recognise their ability to develop into spiritual leaders.

4. They would live with the people whenever they were welcomed, exchanging teaching and medical assistance for food and shelter.

5. They would stay out of controversies between people in the lowlands and the tribes, but do what they could to help tribal people secure their rights as equal citizens.

But, except for the Mangyan who lived in the fringe areas, they still knew so little about them. Where exactly were the other groups located? Thanks to the pioneer work of Marie Barham and Frances Williamson, and now Hazel Page, they were getting more information about the Iraya and Buhid Mangyan, and they were aware of the southern-most Hanunoo. The Alangan seemed to be mixed in with the Iraya, and there were reports of other groups of that tribe further into the interior. But what about the Tawbuid, that mysterious group that nobody had ever seen? And the Tadyawan—where would they find them?

The new candidate group quickly caught Jim's vision for reaching the Mangyan. They could see the wisdom of the principles he laid out for the work, and most of all they were impressed with his compassion—for the Mangyan, certainly, but also compassion for them. They knew that he regarded them as God's chosen instruments to work his plan for reaching the tribes and affectionately dubbed him 'Dr B'—their supervisor, but also their father figure.

Two survey trips helped to set the direction of the work. One came when Jim Broomhall and Russell Reed accompanied Marie Barham on a trek into a Buhid village on the east side. During the nine-mile hike through jungle growth and burned-over fields and up and down one mountain ridge after another, Marie's stamina amazed the two men. Her glasses perched no-nonsense on her round nose, and wearing a sensible cotton dress, she appeared to have boundless energy. In the remote village they found the people living in shabby huts and covered with sores and huge ulcers from yaws, a condition caused by an organism in the ground and made worse by poor hygiene. These Buhid seemed bewildered by the message of the gospel recordings Marie had brought with her, though she had visited them before and the recordings were supposedly in their language. How could they be sure they were communicating in the dialect of any one group of people?

Early in the summer Jim enlisted Russell to go with Hazel Page to visit the Mindoro National Agricultural School ten miles inland from the eastern coastal road. There they met Mangyan from the Alangan tribe who had come across the mountains to trade. Russell returned elated with the possibility that the school might be a central location for reaching some tribes that had still not been contacted—especially the Tawbuid, a group that seemed to elude everyone.

Weeks later, when the new group finished their Tagalog study, they received their work assignments. Barbara and Russell could scarcely contain their joy. The Tawbuid! They were assigned to a group of Mangyan that no one had even seen in the year they had spent on Mindoro. Jim Broomhall agreed that the agricultural school would make a good base location. When permission came from school authorities for them to live in one of the houses on the grounds, the Reeds left Calapan for their first field home: a little Nipa-palm hut.

Northern Mindoro, 1954

Under the careful supervision of Miss Page and Miss Williamson (as the newer missionaries respectfully called them), Caroline Stickley, the secretary from Pennsylvania, and Joy Hayman, the 'MK' from Australia, were getting their first experience of 'real' missionary life while continuing their study of Tagalog.

For one or two weeks Joy would go with Hazel Page up to the Mangyan village of Kaagutayan where they helped teach a small nucleus of interested Mangyan and worked on their Tagalog while Hazel collected words for an Iraya dictionary, the first step in communicating the gospel to the Iraya hidden in the forest areas. During that time Caroline and Frances Williamson lived in the house by the sea in San Teodoro, held religious classes in the government school, taught and encouraged believers in the town, and worked on the new Iraya words they had collected the week before when it was their turn to be in the village. The following week Caroline and Joy would swap locations and senior missionaries. Already these young women had lightened the load, and the older missionaries looked forward to the time when they could expand their outreach. Before long, the first opportunity came.

The Mangyan in a village further inland had heard about the missionaries and asked that they come there and teach the 'new religion' in the government school in the town. Bayanan was nestled up against Mount Halcon, Mindoro's highest mountain. Hazel and Frances began taking turns travelling there once a week and teaching the children in the school during religious instruction time.

On one of Hazel's trips to Bayanan, she took the old wooden bus to the end of the road, and, as usual, one of the men from the village met her and carried her pack on the two-hour hike to the school. Teaching the children that day with their shining dark eyes and shy smiles, Hazel wondered if any of the teaching about the true God and his Son, Jesus, was getting back to the parents. She and Frances had talked with the adults of the village, but they hadn't been able to spend time teaching them.

When her classes were over that day, some of the leaders of the village approached her. Their quiet demeanour gave little hint of the importance of their request. 'Come and live here with us so we can learn God's teachings like the children are learning them.'

Hazel's delight at hearing this request was tempered by a practical matter. 'If you will provide me with a house, I'll come,' she said. 'How long would it take for you to find me a house?'

'Oh, we have one now,' said the leaders. 'It needs a little repair, but you can move in today.' That was sooner than Hazel could manage, so she arranged to go back to San Teodoro, get her belongings, and return in a few days to make this her new home. When she returned some of the men added more palm leaves to the half-walls of her six-by-eight-foot house and repaired the rickety porch. She noticed that the bamboo floor slats ran the long way. For someone with her height, it made sleeping on them more comfortable.

From the first day there, Hazel knew that God had gone before her, preparing many of these people to receive the message. Surely he had something important in mind for this village of obviously seeking Mangyan? Sometimes they would crowd inside her tiny one-room house, spill over onto the porch, and listen to gospel recordings the entire day. On Sundays they wanted not just one, but two meetings to hear Hazel read Bible stories from the Tagalog New Testament and lead them in prayer.

One of the oldest residents of Bayanan was a bow-legged woman named Grandma Bulaklak ('flower'). Hazel watched the old woman's face come alive with emotion as she listened to Hazel tell the story of Jesus. Hazel didn't realise that this was not the first time Grandma Flower had heard the good news.

Before the turn of the century when Spain still ruled the Philippines, a young Filipino had found his way to the village of her people and told them about Jesus. Before he could teach them very much another group began to harass him and he left the area. After that no one else had come to help them understand his message.

As the wrinkled old woman listened again to the gospel stories the memories of that time returned. Even as a child she had sensed that what the Filipino told them was truth. With the joy of recognition she exclaimed, 'Why, this is the same Jesus!' Before long several others, including the village leaders, also believed.

The people in Bayanan seemed concerned for Hazel's well-being, especially since her house was off the path outside the village. Most nights they sent a couple of children from the village to stay with her and keep her company. On one of the nights when the children hadn't come, Hazel suddenly woke from a sound sleep.

It was the voices that woke her–men's voices, several of them. They sounded angry and brash and . . . yes, as though they were drunk. She thought that all the men in the village had left to work on a government job, but she recognised the voice of one of them. What were they saying? As the men neared her house she could make out a few words.

'. . . kill her . . . see if there's a God or not . . .'

Hazel sat up on her mat, knowing there was no

place to hide. She was vulnerable, alone, and without a weapon in her house. Too far from the village for a scream to be heard.

The voices were closer now. She peered through the open wall into the black night. 'Lord, I'm in your hands,' she prayed.

Suddenly the voices stopped–silence–then the sound of feet running away from her house towards the village. Hazel waited, straining for audible signs of their return, but only familiar sounds filtered through the night–a dog barking, a small animal creeping through the brush behind the house, the wind lightly flapping palm branches.

With a grateful prayer, she lay down on her mat and fell asleep.

In the morning a woman from the village visited her. Hazel recognised her as the mother of one of the men whose voices she'd heard in the darkness. The woman seemed to know about Hazel's experience. 'Were you afraid last night?'

'Yes, I was,' Hazel answered, 'but I remembered that the Bible says, "When I am afraid I will trust in the Lord."'

'Do you know why the men didn't hurt you?' the woman asked. 'Because of those two large people dressed in white, standing on each side of the path to your house. The men were afraid to go past them.'

CHAPTER SEVEN

Our village has moved again. This time it's to a place further up the mountain and far from the river. But there is a good stream nearby, so we will have water. I can see some children coming from the stream now, carrying short bamboo tubes full of water for the evening meal.

It was because of the children that we moved. They were not safe. In the village below us, while the parents were gone, police came and took two children away to live at the government school in town. They just took them! The government says all of our children must go to school. They have built a house where all the children live while they are away at the school. But we want them to be with us, and we need them to care for the little ones while we are working in the sweet potato fields. Tell me, how does the school help them understand Mangyan ways? That is what's important.

Before the last typhoon a child from another village

near here died at the government school. Her parents
didn't even know she was sick. She was dead before they
told the parents anything.

Now I'll tell you a secret, but very softly so the spirits
can't hear . . . my wife and I will have a child of our
own before the next harvest.

Bayanan, Mindoro, 1954

After her close call with the night visitors, Hazel's
Bayanan friends moved her to a house in the village. One night she and the children who were
staying with her had just finished their bedtime
Bible story when the mother of one of them
came running up to the house, out of breath.
'Grandma Flower said to ask you what to do,' she
said. 'We're very afraid because evil spirits have
chased people on the path to the village. Thirteen
years ago when this happened many in the village
died afterwards–killed in the Japanese invasion.
What shall we do? Should we run up into the mountains? Can Jesus help us?'

'Go and call the others to come here and we will
talk to Jesus about it,' said Hazel.

Soon over thirty people from five families stuffed
themselves into her little house, some of them carrying bundles of their belongings, already poised to
flee. 'How can I make them see your strength,
Lord?' she prayed, watching them find places to sit
on the crowded floor. She could see the eyes darting
nervously to the doorway, and the muscles tensed

for action. Her heart ached for these people so bound by fear. Some seemed to relax when she picked up her Tagalog Bible and began to read verses that demonstrated God's power. Then she led them in a prayer, asking that God would protect them and bring them his peace.

'Are you still afraid?' she asked after the prayer.

'No, I'm not,' said some of them. Others nodded, still not convinced.

'Remember, if you want God to answer your prayer, you must ask him to forgive your sins. Have you done that?' she asked.

'Oh yes, I have,' said a few of them. Others answered, 'No, I haven't,' but they wanted to do this now, so Hazel led them in simple prayers of repentance.

'Now, everyone who is not afraid should go home and have a good sleep,' she said. 'The others can stay here with me and we will talk more about Jesus.'

Two hours after the first alarm had sounded, all of the villagers who had come to her had left, reassured of God's protection, and Hazel lay her own head down, her heart beating joyfully to realise what God had done that night.

The next morning grateful village friends visited, bringing her gifts of corn and sweet potatoes. As she heard their reports of peaceful sleep, she stopped to praise God with them. It was clear that Satan would not let these people go without a fight, but surely God had prepared them for some special reason.

What part would Bayanan play in his plan to reach the Mangyan tribes?

In the autumn of 1954 Caroline Stickley joined Hazel at Bayanan. Since she'd arrived, Caroline had searched and finally found a perfect place to be alone to pray—a huge rock in the middle of a narrow river near the village. Today she sat on the rock watching the water swirl around its base. Here she could drink in the beauty of God's word, surrounded by the beauty of his creation. Sometimes she would sing hymns triumphantly, at the top of her voice, accompanied by the crashing of the water coming down from the mountain above her. She had sung one today: 'Great is thy faithfulness, O God my Father. There is no shadow of turning with thee.' At the end of the chorus, where the notes rise dramatically, Caroline held them long and made them soar up to the top of the cliffs above the river. The Mangyan told Hazel to warn Caroline about the rock. 'She must stay away from the rock,' they said. 'Evil spirits live there.' Maybe she had proved something about the power of God by continuing to come out here.

Hazel had shared the story of her close call the night the men came to her house. Caroline thought about what this meant. An angel guard! Just like the time God sent an angel to get the disciple Peter out of prison, God had sent angels to guard Hazel. A few days later, Hazel said, she received a letter from her mother saying that because of unexplainable concern, both her mother and her prayer partner back home had prayed for her at the very time she was in danger.

Caroline thought about how the Lord had arranged for a way to reach the areas further up the mountain–through the Mangyan themselves. Grandma Flower and some of the others had begun to travel up to the more remote areas to spread the good news, sometimes walking more than ten hours.

Not long ago, leaders from the Alangan tribe who had been visited by these Iraya Mangyan 'missionaries', came down from their village of Ayan Bekeg on the slopes of Mount Halcon. They asked Hazel and Caroline to come and stay with them and teach them. The first time they visited Ayan Bekeg, after the guide had led the two of them across a swinging bridge that stretched from the cliffs above one side of the river to the footpath on the other side, and they had climbed the track worn into the side of the mountain–almost straight up, it seemed–they came to the edge of the village. Someone must have warned the people of strangers, because she and Hazel could see some of them running out of their houses and disappearing into the forest. Gradually they had crept back and eventually everyone crowded into one of the houses to hear the gospel recordings. It looked as though the chief would be the first to believe. He was surely impressed with what 'the big black book' said. The shaman also seemed keenly interested.

The water rushed past her rock and Caroline grinned. Here she was, the girl who had been afraid of water and thought she'd die by drowning on that first ocean voyage. Now she sat surrounded by water—and she lived on a little island way off somewhere surrounded by more water. God must have a sense of humour.

Mindoro National Agricultural School, East Mindoro, 1954

Barbara and Russell Reed celebrated Christmas in their nipa-palm and pole hut at the agricultural school. Yesterday, Christmas Day, it had rained non stop and through the night. Today it had continued to pour. This kind of weather could make it difficult to trek into the back country. After numerous trips into the surrounding area, Russell still had made no headway discovering where the Tawbuid lived. He and Barbara weren't really discouraged—yet.

Today their immediate concern was their safety as they watched the creek near the house grow into a raging river. They could see logs being swept downstream as though they were mere corks. The rain continued all day and into the night while they lay side by side in their sleeping bags and prayed for the Lord's protection for them and for little Ricky, who slept peacefully in his corner. They wondered if the others still there at the agricultural school during the Christmas vacation were OK, and included them in their prayers. Maybe it would have been safer for them to have taken one of the four empty student huts in the centre of the compound. Being near the creek had its advantages, but not in a storm like this.

About three o'clock in the morning they woke to

the sound of water rushing beneath their house and the dull thud of logs striking the foundation poles as they swept by. It sounded as though the water flowed just beneath the bamboo floor slats. Russell switched on the flashlight. In its powerful beam they could see rapidly-flowing water all around them, several feet deep and as wide as the field behind them. Just in time, Russell rescued their ladder stairs floating away from the house. Where could they go for higher ground? Again they prayed for protection and tried to go back to sleep. Would the water rise above the five-foot poles–and what would happen if it did?

A sawmill in North-east Mindoro, 1955

After three days of hiking under a broiling sun, Hazel and Caroline sat, exhausted, hoping for a lift. Behind them the sign on the wooden building announced it was the office of the sawmill located out here in the forest. Perhaps a truck from the nearby lumber camp would arrive soon and they could hitch a lift. Otherwise it would be a nine-mile walk to their next destination.

This was not the first time Caroline and Hazel had strapped on their army packs this spring and set out to search for the Tadyawan tribe on the east side of the island. In the three years since Frances Williamson and Marie Barham first arrived, the Mindoro team had made at least some contact with three of the six Mangyan tribes. In the south,

New Tribes Mission had begun to work with the Hanunoo, considered the most advanced Mangyan. That left the Tawbuid and the Tadyawan to be contacted. Somewhere off these interior tracks there must be Tadyawan. But where were they?

Hazel thought of Marie and her cheerful attitude even though she spent much of her time just learning the Buhid language and still had no house where she could stay in any of the villages she visited. Having two other missionaries with her for a few months to take over part of the work had freed her to visit areas further south, but it still seemed that the proud and aloof Buhid were simply tolerating her attempts to communicate. Lisigan, the language helper Marie hoped would be the first Buhid believer, blew hot and cold. He and the other Buhid were afraid that believing the Christian message would mean coming 'within the fence of civilisation', as they put it, and if they did, there would be another world flood. They had their own version of the great flood. They believed that two kinds of people divided the world. On one side were people 'outside the fence' who used paper and pencil, went to school, and approved of gambling, fighting and killing. On the other side, 'inside the fence', were the Buhid.

The work among the Iraya tribe encouraged everyone. In Kaagutayan eighty people (including visiting missionaries and a few Filipino Christians) gathered to dedicate the first Mangyan church building on the island. Frances' language assistant,

Anghel Anias, and the new believers in the village decided to build the church while Frances nursed a sprained ankle in Manila. Built of small tree trunks, palm leaves and bark, it fitted in naturally with the homes lined up beside it.

And what would they have done without the new missionaries, like Caroline here–and Morven? Morven Brown, recently arrived from New Zealand, now worked with Hazel in the Alangan village of Ayan Bekeg several miles up the mountain above Bayanan. The Alangan there sometimes listened for six hours at a time to the Tagalog gospel recordings. When they realised they could have recordings in their own language as soon as they helped Morven and Hazel learn it, they began seriously teaching the two missionaries. During this process, several had become believers.

Hazel stretched her long legs. Maybe they should start walking again. Suddenly, down the trail in front of them, four strongly built Mangyan in loincloths appeared, walking down the path towards the saw-mill office. They stopped abruptly when they saw the women. Slowly, trying not to scare them, Hazel and Caroline got up and began walking towards them, smiling, and greeting them in Tagalog. One of the men hid behind another who seemed less afraid. This one's teeth were rotted and irregular, and his crossed eyes seemed even more noticeable because of the thick hair that sprouted uncontrollably from his head. 'Have you heard of "our Father" up in heaven?' Caroline asked. There was no response.

'Our Father is the one who made everything, even you,' she continued. Still the men only stared.

'How much did your shoes cost?' asked the brave one.

'Four pesos,' said Hazel, then quickly added, 'Would you like to hear some of our Father's words?' Not waiting for an answer she opened the phonograph, wound it quickly, and put on a record in Tagalog.

The phonograph and the sound seemed to captivate the men. Hazel changed to a tribal language record. Would they understand it? The men's facial response told them that the Mangyan understood. But when they asked, 'Did you understand?' the leader said, 'No. We're going now,' and left as quickly as they'd come.

It seemed like just another brief encounter with the Mangyan. It would be five years before Caroline would know the importance of this day in God's plan for the Mangyan tribe known as Tadyawan.

CHAPTER EIGHT

You will be surprised when I tell you what the spirits did today. We were working in the field outside the village when I noticed that the birds had stopped singing and the sky looked strange. Something wasn't right. My brother said, 'Why is it getting dark like it is the end of the day? There is no storm coming.'

I was frightened. Everyone was, even the dogs—we could hear them howling in the village. Soon it became like night. You could see the sun, but it looked like a dark ball with a small red light around the edge. We began to whisper to each other, 'Very powerful spirits are confusing the day and they are angry. What should we do?'

Two of the men began to chant to the spirits, asking them to make it light again and promising to sacrifice a pig after the harvest. The spirits must have been pleased, because after a while it began to get light.

Later, I remembered my wife. Her time was coming very soon and maybe the spirits made trouble for her in the great darkness. I ran back to the house and found my mother there cooking rice. She lifted her chin towards the corner. There was my wife sitting against the wall, holding a baby! I wrapped the birth cord in a leaf and tied it high in a tree by the field so the child will grow up to be a hard worker and find a good husband.

My wife thinks that good spirits sent the darkness because it brought us a healthy baby daughter. Maybe she is right.

OMF candidate school, 1955

Almost two years after posting her application to OMF, Bev Erickson joined the other American applicants in Philadelphia for the spring 1955 session of candidate school. With a year of additional experience in evangelism under the Canadian Sunday School Mission (as requested by OMF), Bev faced the next months of preparation with determination.

She hadn't anticipated, however, the 'Emily Post' lectures the women candidates were required to attend. Nor did she expect preparation for the mission field to include knowing how to serve a real English tea. This emphasis on propriety made Bev and the other American women especially nervous of meeting their English counterparts when they sailed to London several weeks later. At the very first meeting in Newington Green, the American girls arrived properly dressed in hats, nylon stockings and high heels. To their surprise, the British girls wore no hats and–bobby socks! Somehow the message about the new OMF 'look' had not been communicated to the States.

Bev had dreamed of the mountains of Mindoro ever since reading a book about the island, *Mountains Singing*. So, at language school in Singapore at the end of the first week of interviews, she joyfully welcomed the recommendation of the directors that she serve on Mindoro. Now the days were filled with Tagalog language study. The two others studying Tagalog, Neville Cooper and Elly van der Linden, were brilliant with language, constantly challenging each other and completing two sections of study in the time it usually took to complete one. Later, in the Philippines, Bev discovered that her tremendous effort to stay at least a respectable distance behind these two, with the kind help of Elly, had put her ahead of her required studies.

After six months in Singapore, the three of them sailed to Manila on a French ship, stopping at the port of Saigon on 1 May where communists showed their strength with a parade of red flags, troops and weapons carriers. In Manila the staff welcomed them at the Philippine headquarters and escorted them on the last leg of their trip to Mindoro. Bev's three foot lockers and two suitcases, mostly full of books and items required on OMF's famous 'outfit list', combined with Neville and Elly's luggage, made travelling a challenge, especially in the sticky month of May.

In Calapan, Dr and Mrs Broomhall welcomed

them warmly, and showed them to the rooms they would occupy during the next phase of language study. Ever thoughtful and efficient, the Broomhalls assigned Elly and Bev to one of the rooms reserved for the senior women missionaries whenever they came into Calapan. Much of the time the new recruits had the room to themselves for language study. When one of the women came in from the field, they shared the room, getting a head start on information and advice about what lay ahead.

Ayan Bekeg, Mindoro, 1955

Whenever she and Morven visited the Alangan, Hazel thanked God for the Christians in Bayanan. They were responsible for the Alangan believers up here on the mountain. On this day the Alangan filled the missionaries' one-room house to capacity. Two women sat on the sagging bamboo floor nursing their babies while others kept an eye on a little army of naked toddlers chasing chickens and showering each other with dirt outside the hut. Their squealing and giggling blended with the cackling of the chickens and an occasional snort from the pig rooting under the house. Hazel had played a gospel recording, and now Mariano Lakoy, the first real believer here in this village, prayed aloud. Hazel loved to hear the Mangyan pray. No matter how halting or short on theological understanding, the prayers were beautiful and real.

Mariano had certainly caught the vision for

evangelism. At Christmas time, when Hazel and Morven made plans for a special celebration, Mariano made plans to share his faith with relatives in another village. 'But you'll miss Christmas,' Hazel told him. 'That's when we thank God for sending us Jesus.'

'Oh, I do that every day,' said Mariano.

The change in the teenage boy sitting near the door amazed Hazel. They'd met Palay, who had been visiting Ayan Bekeg with relatives, earlier in the week. He'd come to the first meeting and backed himself into a far corner. His face was dirty, his curly hair matted and dusty, but he listened as though his life depended on it. The next day, all clean with hair smoothed, he shyly told them that he believed God's message as soon as he heard it the day before. They started teaching him to read and could tell he was very bright. Both she and Morven wondered what would happen to him when he left the village with his relatives tomorrow.

There was much to be done and few missionaries to cover all the areas, especially when it took hours to hike from one place to another. Thank God for the Mangyan who were spreading the good news on their own. But these people needed solid teaching to help them stand up to demonic power. That power already confused some of the new believers who so easily fell back into spirit worship, usually when someone became ill.

The afternoon sun filtered through the woven palm branches of the sloping roof, making Palay squint as he listened to Morven tell the Bible story. 'He's yours, Lord,' Hazel prayed. 'Take care of him.'

Ligaya, south-west Mindoro, 1956

On the other side of the island, Barbara and Russell Reed settled into their new home. Much had happened since that alarming night at the agricultural school, and now, listening to her neighbours, Barbara realised that once more God had saved them from harm. She listened with heart pounding to their discussion of the latest news in the little seaport of Ligaya. The *San Nicholas*, the small motor boat that just this week had refused to take them to the new location here on Mindoro's west coast, had sunk last night. They could have been on it! Instead, here she was, keeping one eye on two-year-old Ricky as she washed out their clothes on the bamboo floor of the porch. The baby, Becky, slept in the other room, while in the kitchen Russell built cupboards from the wooden boxes that had brought in their food supplies.

Barbara wondered how many times God had diverted disaster when they weren't even aware of it. She thought of the flood at the agricultural school. She had to admit feeling afraid, listening to the water swirl around their house. They were relieved when the rain stopped the next morning, but the water was still high. Then that old woman from across the school compound came sloshing through the field with four dozen eggs and some rice and bananas to sell. How did she make it through all that water? They heard from her that the four student huts in the centre of the compound were swept away by the flood. And they thought they might have been better off in one of those during the storm!

She recalled the time Ricky was almost strangled by his cot harness. Something had made her leave her pan of washing beside the creek and run back to the house where he had been sleeping peacefully when she left. She was just in time; he had already begun to turn blue.

Now their prayers were being answered for the Tawbuid. At least Russell had actually met some—more than two years after they first arrived in the Philippines! They'd hoped to find them while they lived at the agricultural school. For six months Russell had explored the area, but not one had been sighted. Then a student from the school told him that the Tawbuid were in the west. So they packed up their belongings and made the exhausting trip by horse cart, bus and boat to the other side of the island. They had arrived at the Mamburao base on the western coast in time to experience the total eclipse of the sun with missionaries there.

They had settled down the coast from Mamburao, and from there Russell walked four hours out to a prison colony hoping to find the Tawbuid. That was another occasion for thanking God for protection because Russell had lost the path and trudged through a swamp before he found his way again. When he got to the prison they told him that dangerous crocodiles lived in the swamp. Again, Russell had seen no Tawbuid.

Soon after this, for the second time in a week, Russell hiked six hours down the coastal track to Ligaya. This time he had a Filipino guide who said there were Tawbuid living near his farm out in the foothills. When Russell came home after that trip, Barbara knew something exciting had happened. She watched his face as he triumphantly handed her a sheet of notes from his pack–Tawbuid words and phrases written phonetically.

He told her how he and the guide had passed the farmhouse and then heard voices on the track ahead. 'It's the Tawbuid,' the guide said. He went ahead to greet them in Tagalog while Russell waited, careful to make no quick movements. Then he saw them– seven men, their loincloths the same dusty clay colour as their skin and hair, with bolo knives hanging from a waist cord. Russell didn't move. One of the men smoked a little clay pipe and another carried a six-inch leaf cone filled with smoking embers. It was the first time they had seen a white man, and if the guide had not reassured them, they would have run away. Because they were on their way to hunt wild pig, the Tawbuid were reluctant to take Russell and the guide to their home, but they finally agreed to it. So, for two hours Russell sat on the floor of their hut and wrote down as many Tawbuid words as he could.

Now that they were here in Ligaya, it would be easier for them to have regular contact with this group of Tawbuid. Barbara watched Ricky making friends with another neighbourhood toddler and hoped that it wouldn't be too long before she and the children would be able to go with Russell out to the Tawbuid village. She could hardly wait.

Bongabon River, south-east Mindoro, 1956

When Marie Barham sailed home to Toronto for a much-needed furlough, she left only half a dozen weak and uncertain Buhid believers. Lisigan, the chief who had been her language teacher, seemed to have completely sold out to the spirits. Before she left he hosted an all-night feast to honour the dead where some of the professing believers joined in the drunken revelry.

Just before Marie's furlough, Bob Hanselman and Joy Hayman, who met at candidate school in Singapore, were married in Manila and then moved into Marie's house in Salcedo. In her absence, the Hanselmans continued the work, using the little they knew of the Buhid language.

Now that she had returned from furlough, the three of them decided to take a day to explore a new area to the south where they hoped to discover Buhid tribes-people. Late in the afternoon they wandered up the wrong stream and were ready to admit defeat when they met a man who told them a Buhid called Daganay lived nearby. 'I'll lead you to his home,' he said.

Daganay welcomed them warmly and Marie explained why they had come. Even though she had prayed that this Buhid would have a prepared and receptive heart, Daganay surprised Marie when he said, 'Yes, we have sin. We need this message.' The Buhid, with a strong sense of self-righteousness, believed that 'sin' meant the fighting, killing, gambling and stealing they saw among the low-landers–actions almost unknown to their culture. But here was a man who seemed to understand the sin that lay deep within.

The openness of Daganay and his family encour-aged the Hanselmans to concentrate their efforts in this area, while Marie continued to use Salcedo as her base. Daganay let them live in a shed near his hut while they visited Buhid in the vicinity. They were unable to stand up in the tiny shed, and they were grateful when Daganay said, 'I can see this house is too small for you. I will build you a house.'

Bob and Joy realised they were now accepted and trusted when they saw their new 'house'–a small addition to Daganay's own hut.

The Hanselmans hadn't known Marie as long as some of the other missionaries, but even they began to notice a change in her energy. Perhaps she didn't rest enough during her furlough–or was discourage-ment sapping her strength?

CHAPTER NINE

My little daughter is walking now. The first time it happened she was sitting on the ground beside our house, trying to reach a chicken pecking in the dirt. When the chicken walked away she squealed and lifted herself right up on her feet and took a couple of steps before she fell. She really wanted that chicken.

My wife and I are happy that the child seems healthy. So many babies die here before they even learn to walk.

We had to hide further up the mountain again yesterday. We heard that the government doctors were in the area looking for people. My cousin says they come with sharp sticks and shove them into your arm. Why would they do that? I remember the Old One said it might be a good thing. Someone told him that it was to keep children from getting sick.

But how do you know? It could be something very bad. I wonder—when the teachers come will they know how to keep my daughter from getting sick?

Passenger Jeeps are always crammed full.

Morning break for Western Tawbuid women in their sweet potato field.

A typical Alangan house in Oriental Mindoro.

*An Alangan woman
and her grandchild
in Oriental Mindoro.*

An Alangan boy peering out of his front door.

A group of Eastern Tawbuid passing the time.

OMF missionaries Ann Flory with Barbara and Russell Reed, 1996 (Ann and Barbara are sisters).

Mariano Lakoy, the first Alangan church leader.

OMF missionary Arlette Dombre from France with Iraya people in North Mindoro.

The Western Tawbuid abandoned this house because someone died there.

A young Western Tawbuid mother.

Western Tawbuid children carry produce down to the lowlands.

The church celebrates a Western Tawbuid baptism.

Bargas, a Western Tawbuid interior leader.

Badyang, north-central Mindoro, 1957

At home in British Columbia for her first furlough after four years in Mindoro, Hazel received a letter from Jim Broomhall asking that she return to Mindoro earlier than she planned for a new assignment that only she could handle. Hazel packed to leave home with mixed feelings. She didn't question the wisdom of the request—she considered her expertise in language a gift of God to be used wherever it was needed—but she regretted cutting short the visit with her family.

Nevertheless, coming back to Mindoro was like coming back to a second family. Not only did her missionary 'family' welcome her, but she also visited one of the villages with part of her Mangyan 'family'. In a few days she would travel down to the south of Mindoro to join Elly van der Linden in work with the Hanunoo tribe. Since New Tribes Mission had graciously turned over to OMF the work they'd begun with the Hanunoo, she and Elly would have their hands full.

Before she joined Elly, Hazel visited the folks at Bayanan and the other places where she had worked with the Iraya and Alangan tribes in past years. In one village where the people had been praying for the Hanunoo tribe for several months, she showed them a photo of the people who would be the centre of her ministry. She was delighted to sense the concern of these relatively new believers that other tribes hear the good news. Down in Bayanan she visited the homes of believers who could read the stories they'd been hearing from the missionaries in the newly published Tagalog Bible.

At a service in another village she watched Palay, now a young married man, stand with his Tagalog Bible and song sheets and lead the group in prayer and hymn singing. What an evangelist he had turned out to be! She could still see that tousle-haired teen-ager sitting in the corner at Ayan Bekeg. Long after she had settled down to sleep that night, Palay and his wife and some of the others sat together singing hymns. The sound was the sweetest of lullabies, for it symbolised the change in these friends who, only two years ago, lived every day in fear of the spirit world.

North-west coast of Mindoro, 1957

It had probably all started with the gangplank. Watching it fall into the sea after the trunks were loaded at the Calapan pier should have told him something.

Canadian Dave Fuller had been part of the Mindoro team for only a few months when Jim Broomhall asked him to accompany the baggage for himself and two missionary women to the far west side of the island. He realised now that it was much more complicated than he'd anticipated. Also, this wasn't exactly what he'd visualised as missionary work when he applied to OMF after graduation from Bible college three years ago. At least it wasn't like the work any of the missionaries described who were regularly welcomed to the Fullers' table during his childhood.

He leaned his wiry body against a dock post and watched the *cargadores* carrying the trunks from the boat he'd arrived on to the one he'd take to get back down to the north-west coast of Mindoro. In his mind he reviewed the plan and absently smoothed back the straight brown hair that barely waved in front over his high forehead and prominent nose. The plan sounded simple at first. He had been assigned to Paluan on the west side of Mindoro for 'consolidation'. This meant that junior missionaries were sent to outstations whenever possible to study the language with a senior missionary while they helped in the work there–an effective on-the-job training programme. There was a simple inexpensive way to get to the west side. You could fly from Calapan to Mamburao on a small DC3 prop plane for only seven pesos. But going by plane left little room for baggage, especially for his own baggage plus the *ten* trunks (he had counted them–twice) belonging to the two women. The plan called for Dave to take all the baggage and go by boat. To do that he would have to sail from Calapan up to Batangas on the south coast of Luzon, and get a small boat to take him around the bay where he'd transfer to another boat to sail down to north-west Mindoro.

At the start of the trip, in Calapan Bay, Dave had just woken from a good nap in a deck-chair when he realised the boat hadn't moved. The captain decided not to sail that day. So Dave returned to the mission home with all the trunks to wait for another boat. Two days later, with the trunks safely aboard, this boat left the pier, but a sudden storm sent them off course to the port where he now waited. In a moment of panic, Dave had wondered what he would do with ten trunks if he missed the connecting vessel. Now, even though the old Chinese junk he'd found reeked of the dried coconut meat called *copra*, at least it sailed in the right direction. Dave found a place on the junk's deck, and let his eyes wander from the deep blue-green of the South China Sea to the brilliant sky overhead. What a beautiful corner of the world–quite different from the beauty of the Canadian landscape he'd grown up with.

In becoming a missionary, he followed the Fuller tradition. Back in 1912 his Methodist preacher dad had brought his bride to Saskatchewan to travel round the prairie circuit, then moved further west for a ministry to shanty men and lumber workers. Just before OMF candidate school, Dave had travelled the railways across Canada for over a year with the Railway Mission of North America, the mission his father had founded after the early days on the frontier. Maybe his dad's pioneer spirit gave him his interest in tribal work.

Suddenly the sputtering of the old junk's motor reminded him that there was still plenty of time for more challenges on this trip. Sure enough, the boat had developed engine trouble. Half way back to Mindoro, they docked for repairs at a small island. Dave paced back and forth, trying to calculate the expenses that still lay ahead. Would his money hold out? Each time the luggage was moved, the peso count mounted. Finally the captain pronounced the ship sailable, and they resumed their trip. Hours later they reached the tiny port on north-western Mindoro. Because of the sloping sand beach the boat had to anchor off shore. Passengers and luggage were transferred to a dug-out canoe with one outrigger that brought them to waist-deep water. Men carried them the rest of the way on their backs.

By this time Dave had negotiated payment for six transfers of luggage and still had to find a way to get all those trunks to Mamburao, several miles across the peninsula on a road where the last typhoon had washed out all the bridges. At each of the four river crossings Dave bargained with a new team of helpers to carry the luggage across on makeshift bamboo bridges. Across the river a vehicle waited to take passengers to the next crossing.

He pulled into Mamburao late that evening, stretching to get the kinks out of his muscles. It had cost him 400 pesos and a days'-worth of careful negotiating to get the baggage there on the money he had with him. For David Fuller the message was clear: patience would be one of the more essential gifts of the Spirit for working on Mindoro.

Calapan, Mindoro, 1958

Jim Broomhall folded the telegram and laid it on his desk. Marie Barham . . . dead. Of course he had known this message would come eventually. When the doctors in Manila operated on Marie and found cancer that had progressed too far, they could only recommend that she go home to Canada. Thank God, Marie had some encouragement with the Buhid work before she left. For her last few months on Mindoro she had lived in a home the Buhid found for her near one of the villages. And in those last months when she was clearly ill, the Buhid had shown new interest in what Marie tried to teach them. They seemed especially fascinated with the concept of prayer.

Jim remembered what some of the Buhid said when they heard Marie was too ill to come back to Mindoro. 'She was like a mother to us. She loved us.' A fitting tribute to this woman who saw only a handful become believers during her time on the island, but spent six years preparing the way for the day when others would see perhaps whole villages of Buhid living under the Lord's banner. Marie was like a John the Baptist, Jim reflected.

'Heavenly Father,' he prayed. 'As thou didst comfort Marie and kept her going in the midst of discouragement, now comfort others here who are bending beneath the load.' Caroline Stickley came to his mind. Ever since Hazel and Caroline met those Tadyawan at the sawmill, efforts to reach the tribe increased. For months Caroline and another woman lived in a rented hut on the edge of Tadyawan territory, hoping to make friends with people from this tribe who passed by on the track near their hut. They'd excitedly reported that the leader of a nearby Tadyawan village agreed to give them an empty house in his village. He seemed to understand that the women had a message about 'our Father in heaven' that they would tell his people as soon as they learned more of the Tadyawan language.

Now, almost a year later, Caroline and her partner had been forced to leave the village. The fear of demons was too strong there. When one of the men became ill, the people believed the demons were angry and would not ask for help from 'our Father in heaven' as Caroline had taught them. The two women could feel interest in the new teaching shrinking and fear of the spirits increasing. When the man died, the group sacrificed a pig to appease the spirits, and soon after decided they didn't want to hear any more of our Father's words. In her report Caroline told how the leader wouldn't look at her when he gave them the final word. Rather, he traced a pattern in the dirt with his finger while he said, 'You may continue to live here, but we plan to move to another mountain.'

So the women had packed up their kerosene stove, their lantern and their cooking pots and said goodbye to these people they'd grown to love. This village had seemed like the perfect base for reaching the Tadyawan further inland. What had gone wrong?

They'd prepared. They'd prayed. 'Show us what thou hast in mind, Father,' Jim prayed. 'Open our eyes to see thy plan to reach these people who need thee so desperately.'

CHAPTER TEN

I'm almost afraid to believe the news that has come from over the mountain. People from a village in the next valley visited us just after we finished planting our fields last week. They say that the teachers have come! They have seen them and talked to them. They are white people, and they have big noses. The teachers know their language and they carry papers they call 'God's words'.

The people in the next valley have built a new house for the teachers. They told us to come there and we could get some teaching from them. We'll leave early tomorrow morning, my wife and I and also my brother. It's only a half-day's walk. The grandmothers will care for our little daughter while we are away.

Tonight I couldn't sleep, so I came out here to think. The moon is so bright I can see the path clearly all the way to where it winds down over the rocks. That's where we'll be heading in the morning when we go to hear the teachers. What do you think they will tell us?

Amnay River valley, west-central Mindoro, 1958

With Hazel Page now working among the Hanunoo, Jim Broomhall assigned Bev Erickson to be Morven Brown's partner at Ayan Bekeg. Bev had no idea that in a few months she and Morven would be making history.

No other villages existed above Ayan Bekeg on Mount Halcon's eastern slopes, but over in the next valley and beyond–all across Mindoro from east to west–there were perhaps thousands of Alangan tribespeople. Russell Reed had seen a few of them on a trek across the Alangan valley several years ago, but he hadn't seen many women and children. Neither had the lumber men who sometimes came through that territory, nor the government people when they sprayed for mosquitoes in their war against malaria. They all assumed that this tribe had an unusually high percentage of men.

In January of 1958 Bev and Morven got the opportunity they had prayed for, when they visited villages in a remote area in western Mindoro. Filipino friends guided them to a fringe area where they surprised a group of Alangan by addressing them in their own language. These people listened intently to the Alangan language records Bev played for them. 'Are you afraid of the evil spirits, darkness, or people who live on the other side of the mountain?' the voice on the record asked. 'Yes!' said one old man who continued to talk back to the phonograph as it played.

Cautiously, the women approached the leader, Presidente, and asked if they could go back into the interior to the main village and bring this message to everyone. Presidente not only agreed, but offered to take them there. As they hiked along with the little man, Bev's joy filled her with new energy. Somehow God had diffused the fear of this fringe group, and they were on their way to Mangyan who had probably never been seen by anyone outside the tribe!

When they arrived in the village, trailing behind Presidente, the people regarded them with expressions of both fear and overwhelming curiosity. While Bev and Morven rested, Presidente directed a shelter to be built on the slope just above the lean-to's the tribe lived in during this hot, dry season. 'You sit there,' he told Bev and Morven, gesturing towards the new shelter.

The two women took their places under the shelter. Just below them sat the village leaders Presidente had invited to come out and hear their message. By the time Bev and Morven began teaching the good news from God's book, the people had relaxed and drank in their words like thirsty travellers. These Mangyan seemed to understand the message and accept it without question—as though they had been prepared beforehand.

That night Bev and Morven lay down on their

mats in the shelter, exhausted but exhilarated, listening to the Alangan mothers singing their peculiar lullabies. In the morning they looked out to see the village already up and ready for the day. Women were cooking a jungle root called *nami* or carrying bamboo tubes of water from the stream. Children were running up the path and playing in the dirt outside the shelters. Watching a baby crawling where a dog and a pig scrambled for a scrap of food, Bev suddenly realised that she could never bring children to a place like this. 'Thank you, Lord. Now I see why you brought me out here as a single woman. I could never come here as a married woman with children. This would be a ministry that families could never have!'

The breakfast of rice and boiled bat reminded Bev of the rhyme that had rolled so easily off her tongue at Bible school: 'Where he leads me I will follow. What he feeds me I will swallow.'

When Bev and Morven reluctantly gathered their packs to leave, they asked Presidente, 'May we come back?'

For a moment their hopes for future ministry with this tribe were dashed when he replied, 'What for? We believe already. You don't need to come back.' But when they showed him the Tagalog New Testament and how much of it he still hadn't heard, he changed his mind.

'OK. Come back then in the spring, before the rainy season.'

In early May, Bev and Morven packed up their

gear to return to Presidente's village. Since their trip there in January an idea had been forming in their minds. Why not attempt something no women had ever done? Why not walk all the way across Mindoro from west to east? They would contact as many Alangan as they could along the way, as well as return to Presidente's village. With packs filled with a kilo of dried fish, a couple of kilos of rice, salt, dried fruit and boiled sweets, plus medicine, blankets, a change of clothes, and mosquito repellent, they started out. Along the way they'd exchange some of their food for whatever the Mangyan would trade, or contribute some of it to the community pot. They could find their way in as far as Presidente's village, and then they would ask him for a guide to the next village, and do the same at each settlement on the track.

When they arrived, Presidente sat holding the side of his head, suffering from a bad headache. Somehow the welcome didn't have the warmth they experienced before. 'Since you left,' he grumbled, 'we have had nothing but sickness,' giving them the distinct impression that this was their fault. Presidente went back to where he'd been lying in the 'bighouse' where at least fourteen members of the tribe were living during the cool season. Bev and Morven played the phonograph and talked with the others. Then they bedded down for the night in their assigned corner of the house, grateful for the smoke hanging over them from the wood fire smouldering in the centre of the room. It would keep most of the mosquitoes away.

Before they fell asleep they heard Presidente's voice. 'My headache is gone. Are those two women asleep?'

Someone answered, 'Yes, they are asleep.'

'I wish they weren't. I want to talk to them.'

With that, Presidente came over and squatted beside Bev. 'Is it true that you want to take this message to all Mangyan everywhere?'

'Yes, that's true,' said Bev, struggling to a sitting position.

'OK. Then I'll send two of my people to take you to the Amnay River. Others will take you on to the next place and the next until you cross the whole valley.' With relief at this welcome news, Bev and Morven listened as Presidente continued.

'It is important that all the people in the valley will see you and know that you really were here the other time.' Spirit beings had been reported in the area—'little people' they called them. When Presidente told people in the valley about the missionaries' previous visit, they didn't believe him, and said, 'It must have been spirits, and not real people.'

Presidente had a more serious concern. 'If you do not get back to your home, the Tagalogs will think we have killed you, and they will come and kill us.' Before they moved on the next morning, Bev wrote a reassuring letter that he could give to the Tagalogs if he should need it.

It took them eight days to cross the island. But

because Bev and Morven spoke their language–and because they were women, women and children did not hide from them as they'd hidden from the men who travelled through here earlier. Along the way, in each Alangan bighouse, there were people who told them they wanted to know more about Jesus, and asked them to return. Morven and Bev knew it would be six months before they could come back. They would have to ask their prayer partners for some powerful intercession for these Mangyan seekers.

Paluan, north-west Mindoro, and Manila 1958

The small porch of the resident missionary's old wooden house in Paluan had been Dave Fuller's home for over a year while he studied Tagalog. Even the Iraya in the nearby hills used that language, so Dave had made trips to those areas as his language facilities improved. The trips helped introduce Dave to tribal work, his goal. Little by little he could see God's plan for him unfolding. He didn't mind what had become a somewhat solitary existence, but he hoped one of these days God would send him someone to share this life. Since he was the only single OMF man on Mindoro, that should give God some advantage.

Jim Broomhall asked Dave to check out a possible new area for evangelism on the Lubang islands off the north-west tip of Mindoro. It would be another one of those roundabout trips–not as complicated, he hoped, as the one when he'd delivered the ten trunks! To get to the islands he'd have to catch a plane from Mamburao to Manila and then a boat to the islands. Dave couldn't leave Paluan until later in the day for the trek down to the Mamburao airstrip, and before he could get there it grew dark–too dark to see the path. Besides that, he felt unusually exhausted. Through the last glimmer of twilight he stumbled on a little shack in a field, and stretched out gratefully on its floor for the night.

In the morning he knew he had one of the worst colds of his life. Feverish and congested, he made his way to the airport and got on the plane to Manila. At the mission home in Manila the couple in charge of the home, Cyril and Doris Weller, welcomed him. Doris, who had been trained as a nurse, said, 'Young man, you aren't going anywhere. You have a very high fever and you should be in bed.' In the absence of a telephone line to the island, Cyril sent a telegram to Jim Broomhall explaining that Dave would complete his assignment as soon as he recovered.

Too ill to argue, Dave let Doris put him to bed in the only place for a single man to recuperate in the over-full house: behind a folding screen near the front door. At least there was no danger of getting lonely in that spot. The Wellers' four young children took care of that.

Dave surprised Bev Erickson when she found him inside the front door of the mission home. She'd come from Calapan to get her glasses mended. That morning when she broke them Jim Broomhall urged her to take the noon ferry so she could get to Manila that day and arrange for their repair. She planned to be in Calapan for several days, so why had Dr B insisted that she go at once?

During the two days in Manila, Bev often dropped in to see if Dave's health had improved. They had become good friends since he'd come to Mindoro and she shared Doris's concern about him. It looked like pneumonia. Before she left to go back to Calapan, Bev stopped to say goodbye to Dave, and discovered that he would be at the OMF vacation house north of Manila the same week she'd be there. For some reason the news disturbed her.

Less than a year later, Bev Erickson and Dave Fuller sat under a palm tree on a hill above Calapan harbour. Further up the hill Jim and Janet Broomhall relaxed under another tree, glad to have a few minutes away from the constant activity down at Ilaya House.

Bev had been in a state of confusion ever since Dave proposed on the last day of their vacation. She felt drawn to Dave, yes, but wasn't she settled in her determination to stay single? Was this relationship something God had arranged or was it a temptation she should resist like the plague? How could she know God's will in this situation? Only Dr and Mrs B and her prayer partner at home knew of her struggle. 'I hope they are praying–really hard,' she thought. The Broomhalls were praying, but they also considered it important to provide a place for the young couple to talk privately while they were in

Calapan without letting the others guess the situation. At this time Jim's days were filled with overseeing the building of the new mission home. Often he would say to Dave, 'I should go up and check out the new property. Want to come along?' Then they'd walk up to the site the back way, over the hill. Janet would say to Bev, 'I need to go to the market for something. Would you like to come along?' They would walk the lower road and eventually end up at the property from the front path off the pier road, where they would meet Dave and Jim.

From up here on the hill you could see way out to the twin islands where ferries chugged through the narrow channel on their way to Batangas. It would be a beautiful place for the new mission home–far enough above the road into town from Calapan pier to be private, but close enough for the sounds and smells of this port town to drift up and keep everyone in touch with reality.

Today, Bev and Dave took little notice of the view. They must make a decision soon. The more-or-less permanent assignments for the Mindoro team were even now being decided. Any one of five single women could be assigned with Bev to a base location, or she could be Dave's partner–for life.

A few weeks later, during breakfast at Ilaya House, the Mindoro group put down their spoons and tea cups and stopped their conversations when Jim Broomhall stood up at the end of the long table.

'After much prayer and deliberation,' he said, 'the following assignments have been made.' Each one there had contributed their own share of prayer for these decisions, knowing that the chemistry and working relationship between field partners could impact ministry for better or worse. Until now Mindoro hadn't had enough field staff for there to be much choice, but now there were several possible combinations, especially among the single women.

Jim read the list: Ann Flory (Barbara Reed's sister) would go with Hazel Page to the Hanunoo, Daphne MacKenzie would join Morven Brown with the Alangan, Carolyn Hanson would go to San Teodoro to work with Frances Williamson—the list went on. Then there was a pause. What about Bev Erickson, some of them wondered. And David Fuller?

'Now. Dave has an important announcement to make,' said Jim, leaving the floor to Dave Fuller. With characteristic charm, Dave announced his engagement to Beverley Erickson, who had finally said 'Yes'. Actually, she had finally said 'No,' because Dave, looking for a new strategy, had asked her, 'Do you have any doubts now?' By that time Bev realised that Dave's presence in her life was part of God's plan. 'No,' she answered.

They didn't see each other again until the Valentine's Day conference in Calapan when Dave presented Bev with the ring he had bought from a Hong Kong mail order catalogue. The night before the conference ended, they stayed up making wedding plans and preparing peanut butter sandwiches for a survey trip Bev would take the next day with two of the other missionaries.

They were married two months later in the lovely garden of the Manila mission home. Bev's mother sent the wedding dress, complete with lace and skirt hoops, and Doris Weller baked a traditional Canadian fruitcake. It tasted delicious even though one of the Weller children had helpfully dumped half a box of soda into the batter.

A few days after their honeymoon north of Manila, Bev and Dave Fuller left for Paluan, the first step on their new journey together.

CHAPTER ELEVEN

Tonight I am very worried as I sit here beside my little daughter. I'm afraid that she will die. Her body is hot and dry and she refuses to eat or drink. She became ill the morning we were to leave to go to hear the teachers, so my wife and I decided to stay with her.

I'm glad we did. Every day she is more sick, and every night some of us gather at the fire pit and sing to the spirits for her. But the spirits are not helping. If she is more sick tomorrow we will have to take her out into the forest and make a place for her there, just like we did for the Old One.

My brother didn't go to hear the teachers either. He started out, but he tripped over a tree root on the path. When that happens, you know that the spirits don't want you to keep going. So he came back to the village.

My wife is afraid now. The shaman in her village forbade the people there to go and hear the teachers. He knew that we planned to go, and she thinks he may have put a curse on our daughter.

If I could see the teachers, I would ask them to help my little daughter. I don't want her to die.

Bayanan, Mindoro, 4 June 1959

Never before had Mangyan from different tribes come together for a joint conference—especially one where the uniting reason was their shared Christian faith. But here in the Bayanan church with its grass roof and absence of walls, Mangyan from three different tribes sat on backless wooden planks and joined their voices in a Tagalog hymn of praise to God who had broken down their barriers of fear and distrust.

Churches in seven areas sent delegates to this first 'Inter-Tribal Believers Conference'. Five Mangyan men led the meetings: Daganay, the Buhid who opened his home to Bob and Joy Hanselman; Palay, the young Iraya man who had scoured the mountains for potential believers; and two other Irayas, Pedro and Francisco, who walked three days to get to the meetings. The fifth leader, Frances Williamson's faithful language assistant Anghel Anias, had limped over the trails to Bayanan and crossed every stream on his wife's back. The ravages of tuberculosis showed on his gaunt face.

Dave Fuller listened while Palay led the group of tribal leaders in prayer. For a moment, the implications of this gathering overwhelmed him. 'This is what it will be like when we worship together in eternity. The body of Christ, united as one. Culture, race, education, physical ability–none of these things divide us. We are one in him.'

For Grandma Flower, sitting with the other women on their side of the church, her tiny body now even more bent with the years, this event was the culmination of years of trekking up and down mountains, trying to get the word out as far as she could. For Dave Fuller and the other missionaries present, it was a little like staying out of the kitchen while your children cooked their first meal. It seemed only yesterday that many of these Mangyan Christians cowered in their villages, afraid to associate with people outside their area, controlled by malevolent, unseen forces. Now they had taken responsibility for this entire conference with missionaries acting only as advisors. The exhausted missionaries may have been tempted to intervene when all five Mangyan leaders preached at each evening meeting, but they would not dampen the enthusiasm of the delegates.

Palay's prayer ended, and someone again requested 'There shall be showers of blessings' from the Tagalog hymnal. Dave suspected that the song's popularity at the conference was partly due to the parched rice fields surrounding the villages during this unusually dry season. In the front row Arnold Lea, OMF's general director, sang along in English. Earlier, he'd brought greetings through an interpreter.

While Anghel Anias limped to the front of the church, Dave again reflected on the afternoon meeting where they'd discussed the possibility of short-term Bible schools. Why not have missionaries come to a central village for three weeks or so and give tribal leaders a firm grounding in the Christian faith? Then the leaders could teach others. Just think—these Mangyan want to be trained to lead their churches! They are willing to take time from caring for their fields and gathering rattan to study God's word.

Dave stood with the others to sing another hymn. Seeing the joy of the Mangyan believers only increased his sense of urgency to reach the rest of the Mangyan throughout the island. This churchful of men and women amounted to only a handful compared to the thousands still waiting to be liberated. Even now, Barbara and Russell Reed were struggling to get through to the Tawbuid. Caroline Stickley and her new partner weren't making much headway with the Tadyawan. There were members of every tribe living in obscure inland areas. How would they reach them? What part would this gathering play in the drama of bringing Christ to the whole Mangyan nation?

Calapan, Mindoro, 1960

Early in the following year, it was no accident that Caroline Stickley and her partner, Dode Pack, were present at the mission home dinner table when a visitor told an interesting story. Russell Glazier had just come from an evangelistic outreach in

Pinamalayan on Mindoro's eastern coast. There he had met a friendly Filipino farmer named Ben who showed no interest in being evangelised. But Ben asked if he knew about some women who could bring this teaching to tribespeople way back in the interior near the Banus River. These tribespeople sometimes worked on Ben's farm and had asked him if he knew about the women teachers. 'I could take the women to where the tribe lives,' Ben said. Glazier promised to check on this for him.

Jim Broomhall watched Dode and Caroline. They had stopped eating and were firing eager questions at Russell Glazier. Where could they find Ben? How soon could he take them to the tribespeople? It sounded like Tadyawan country. This could be the break they'd been praying for! Until now the team had found only a few Tadyawan scattered here and there with interest high at first, but so far no group showed enough interest to request 'live-in' missionaries. Now here was a group that said, 'Come and teach us.'

The very next morning Caroline and Dode hopped aboard the red wooden bus to Pinamalayan. They found Ben and made arrangements for him to guide them into Tadyawan country.

They started out with Ben early the following morning, hiking up the path beside the Banus river winding between shadowy blue-green mountains and beside rice fields ready for harvest. The clear sunny day matched their mood. But they progressed slowly even where the walking was easier because

Ben knew most of the farmers they met along the way. Each deserved a friendly chat and a swig out of the bottle he carried with him. By noon it seemed as though another river crossing appeared before Caroline and Dode could shake the tiny pebbles out of their canvas shoes from the last one they'd waded across. Then they were stumbling down the river bed itself, their energy melting under the relentless sun. They barely noticed the lush scenery of this river valley.

By late afternoon the two women came face to face with the day's biggest obstacle—a rocky cliff rising straight up from the other side of the river. They followed Ben across huge boulders rising out of the river and then stared up at the formidable face of the cliff. They had been bone-weary to the point of tears while following the river bed. How could they ever climb up the side of a cliff? With prayer and bare feet, Caroline decided, removing her shoes, tying the laces together and hanging them around her neck. Every toe-hold and finger anchor was a challenge as she inched her way around the bare face of the cliff, with Dode following. She didn't have to glance down too many times at the jagged rocks below for motivation to make it to the top.

Finally, their limbs weak and rubbery with the strain, Caroline and Dode scrambled over the crest to a welcome sight. Ben's farm, where the Tadyawan waited for them, lay just ahead. They could see the house in the dusky light.

They changed into dry clothes in the tall grass

near the house, and then went inside where at least forty Tadyawan huddled on the floor of the main room. Ben and the Filipino farmer talked while Caroline and Dode sat on the floor and waited. The tribespeople seemed shy and afraid. None of them said anything.

Then Caroline saw a familiar face–bushy, uncontrollable hair, crossed eyes, and crooked, rotting teeth. Of course. It was the man she and Hazel met at the sawmill when they were doing the survey. That must have been five years ago! The tribesman saw Caroline looking at him and said to Ben, 'I know her.'

With that, the Mangyan relaxed and the room came alive with chatter. They were formally introduced to Pedro, the man Caroline recognised in the crowd. Then, in a mixture of Tadyawan and Tagalog, Dode and Caroline told this now-eager group about 'our Father in heaven' and why Jesus had come to earth. They talked long into the night, forgetting their aching limbs in the glow of this roomful of people who seemed strangely prepared for the gospel message.

Bayanan, Mindoro, 1960

The soft 'chink' of steel hitting earth and stone blended with the sound of cockerels crowing and children calling in the village below. Frances Williamson stood on the hilltop near a stand of tall fern with a group of Mangyan friends from the

Bayanan church. They watched the hole in the packed clay ground widen under the knives and pickaxes of three of the men. One of the men picked up a piece of rattan and measured the length of a small form wrapped in split bamboo lying near the hole. He measured the hole, nodded to the others, and they gently lifted the form and laid it in the hole. Then, as clumps of earth were dropped back into the opening, the group began to sing in Tagalog, 'Blessed assurance, Jesus is mine. Oh, what a foretaste of glory divine.'

'Grandma Flower is now tasting that divine glory.' Frances choked back a lump in her throat, realising that she would never again watch that angular figure struggle up the mountain path or see her wrinkled old face appear in the doorway to say, 'I have a question to ask you.' The tiny woman couldn't read the Scriptures herself, and her questions often reflected her touching desire to please God with every part of her life. 'What does God's book say?' she would ask.

Frances pictured the welcoming committee of Mangyan who had gone on to 'glory' before Grandma Flower. Some would be ones who were there because of this dear granny's untiring efforts to spread the word up and down the mountains of northern Mindoro.

'This is my story, this is my song: praising my Saviour all the day long.' As Frances followed the group back down to the village, the words of the last chorus hung in the air, a beautiful eulogy for Grandma Flower.

South Mindoro, 1960

Down in Hanunoo country Hazel Page broke in a new recruit. Barbara Reed's sister, Ann Flory, tramped behind the tireless Hazel on a track that would soon lead them to another group of Mangyan, mysteriously ready to accept Christian teaching.

Hazel had developed a regular route of villages to visit, carrying in simple medicines and her big black Tagalog Bible. As usual, her heavy pack also included food, Coleman pressure lamp, dishes–whatever she'd need to survive several days on the route.

Today she and Ann headed towards a village by the sea–one Hazel had never before visited. Dogs barking and the laughter and shouts of children told them they were almost there. Hazel could see Ann's weary face light up when she heard the children. She'd noticed that in every village on the route Ann gathered the children around her. With her teaching background she knew how to relate to them, and even with her limited knowledge of the tribal language, children responded to her efforts to communicate.

Nearing the village, they could see evidence of the recent earthquake and tidal wave that had ravaged this stretch of seaside. As they greeted the people grouped in tight little clusters around the village, they sensed the fear that still gripped this Mangyan tribe.

The village leader invited Hazel and Ann to meet

with some of his people. Hazel lifted the Tagalog Bible from her pack and sat down on the ground in front of the leader. His eyes fastened on the book. 'Is that the book the spirits told us about?' he asked.

In answer, Hazel carefully summarised some of the Bible's teachings. Then the leader said, 'Yes! That's what we were told. Our ancestors said someone would come with a big black book and tell us the way to life.'

Then Hazel explained God's provision for eternal life. Some of the people wept gratefully. Others said, 'This is the way. This is what we heard. Yes, we want to follow this way.'

'How extraordinary!' Hazel pondered what they witnessed here today. Could it be that God had prepared these people through their ancestors to receive his message?

CHAPTER TWELVE

I have good news! Remember the day my little daugh-
ter was so sick? My wife and I decided that we would
look for a sign. If she did not die, we would go to see the
teachers. But if she died, we would know that the spirits
were angry and we shouldn't go.

The next morning her body was cool, and she asked
for water. The following day she was able to sit up, and
in four days she was running after the chickens again!

So my wife and I travelled down to the place where
the teachers were staying. My brother didn't go. He's
still afraid.

The teachers have good words. They told us about
God who made this forest and made us too. He has
more power than the spirits and he won't trick us or
scare us. Do you think this is true? I would like to
believe this teaching. I wish the Old One was here.

Banus River, 1961
Ligaya, south-west Mindoro, 1961

To the west of Hanunoo country, Ann Flory's sister and brother-in-law, Russell and Barbara Reed, packed for a trip that would shed new light on the past six discouraging years. Although they had found a small village of the elusive Tawbuid tribe, they had made almost no headway in their evangelistic efforts. At first the tribe seemed friendly enough. They even allowed Russell and Barbara to stay for short visits in an abandoned house in the village. Barbara developed a special friendship with one of the village women. But no one, except perhaps one old grandfather, responded to the message.

The tragedies with this group began when an almost-blind pregnant woman tripped against a jagged tree stump, puncturing her abdomen and killing her unborn baby. Russell arrived at the village days later and found it deserted. He searched the surrounding area and found the group in a new place, almost paralysed by fear after three more of their people had died from a mysterious disease similar to pneumonia. One of them was Barbara's friend. Days later, another man died, and then a woman died with no symptoms except stark fear. The people huddled in two tiny huts, the doorways and cracks in the walls stuffed with branches and leaves so the demons couldn't enter and kill them too. At night they kept a fire burning and were afraid to sleep. They abandoned the fields of those who died. They refused to listen to what Barbara and Russell tried to tell them about Jesus who could take away their fear.

Now Jim Broomhall had written, asking the Reeds to visit eastern Mindoro where Caroline Stickley and Dode Pack had begun work among the Tadyawan near the Banus River. The Tadyawan had built a large house by the river for the women to live in while they taught tribespeople coming in from around the area. Lately some Tawbuid who used the same river route had begun to show an interest when the new Tadyawan believers, who spoke some Tawbuid, told them what they were learning. One of their leaders asked if people who spoke Tawbuid could come and teach them as well.

So there were Tawbuid on the east side! Russell had spent months searching for them while they were living at the agricultural school, but never that far south. Why had it taken this long to find them? Why didn't God lead them there six years ago? Sometimes it seemed as though the only thing they had really done in their years on Mindoro was learn the Tawbuid language. Full of questions, the Reeds delivered their two children to Manila for the next school term. Then, back on Mindoro, they met Caroline and Dode at their base in the coastal town of Pinamalayan.

Caroline, still excited about their last trip to visit the Tadyawan, told what had happened. Their cross-eyed, bushy-haired friend, Pedro, said that a Tawbuid named Tiban had been greatly influenced by his father's prophetic dream about strangers coming with good teaching. That dream seemed to be a factor in the Tawbuid's desire for teaching. 'Then, guess what Pedro said,' Caroline continued. 'He said that years ago someone in the Tadyawan tribe had a vision similar to that dream. An angel appeared to this tribesman and told him that some day people from another land—strange-looking, but good people, would come and bring them good teaching. The angel told him that they should all listen to the teaching and follow it. Pedro told me, 'That's why we were all waiting for you!''

The implications of Caroline's story overwhelmed Barbara and Russell. Could it be that God had been preparing these people for years and years to hear the gospel?

The four of them rode in one of the brightly decorated, stretched-out jeeps called jeepneys to the end of the road and continued the rest of the way by foot. When they reached the grass-roofed house by the river, Tiban's group was not there. But the next day several other Tawbuid appeared at the house. They grinned when Russell played the recordings he and Barbara had made with Tawbuid speakers from the west, but obviously the eastern Tawbuid had a different dialect. While the two of them tried to figure out the difference in language, they discovered that these Tawbuid had a word for a good spirit who had been involved in creation: *Funbalugu*.

Barbara and Russell returned to their home in

Ligaya wondering if the trip had been worth it. The few Tawbuid they'd met seemed interested, but, just as in the west, they didn't appear to accept the message.

More disappointment came when they visited their Tawbuid friends in the hills and discovered that another cruel pagan custom had been followed– a newborn baby's life had been extinguished because the father died before its birth. On the next visit the people were again clutched by fear after the death of a sixteen-year-old boy. They could hear the clacking of the bamboo sticks to scare away the spirit of the dead boy before they reached the village. The Tawbuid had already lost the proceeds of their entire rice harvest when they used it to purchase ten pigs to sacrifice in a full-moon ceremony to placate the spirits of the people who died earlier. Now they sacrificed another pig for the dead boy's spirit in a midnight ceremony and feast. Those who had listened to the new teaching knew this conflicted with what the Reeds taught them, but their deeply ingrained fear kept them from giving up what had been part of their lives for as long as they could remember.

A few months later a letter from Jim Broomhall encouraged them to consider a second trip to the east. 'Surely something is happening among the Tawbuid in this area,' Caroline had reported to him, 'and someone should make a concentrated plunge into the area.'

This time when the Reeds crossed the last bend of

the swift Banus River with *Caroline* and *Dode*, they were greeted by a crowd of smiling, staring Mangyan standing in front of a much larger house. Caroline explained that half of the palm-thatched house had been built by the Tadyawan and half by the Tawbuid. 'And these are the Tawbuid,' said Caroline, indicating a group of at least thirty Mangyan crowding in to get a closer look at the new missionaries. Caroline introduced the Reeds to Tiban, their leader, the one who had been so influenced by his father's dream. Tiban escorted the Reeds into the new house and over to a six-foot platform about eighteen inches high with a split bamboo floor—the section usually reserved for tribal leaders.

The Tawbuid sat quietly watching Russell and Barbara unpack their supplies and roll out their sleeping bags on the platform floor. Russell could tell that they expected their first lessons from God's book tonight. He sat down on the platform and began with the first of the series of lessons he and Barbara had carefully put together for this meeting. The group gathered in front of them seemed to listen with every fibre of their being. Why were these Tawbuid different from those in the west, and even different from the eastern Tawbuid they'd met earlier?

Less than a week after the Reeds arrived, they sat on logs outside the river house with Tiban discussing the meaning of *Funbalugu*. Tiban began to talk about his father's dream.

'My father told me that a new teaching would

come into the interior. When it came I must listen and obey it.' Tiban shifted his position on the log. 'Only a half-month after he told me that, my father died. He wasn't even sick.' Tiban explained that, true to Tawbuid custom, he had taken this last charge from his father as 'law'. A few months ago when he heard that two white women had come into the Banus area with a new teaching, he and some others went down to check it out. The teachers spoke Tadyawan, interpreted as well as they could by Tadyawan who spoke Tawbuid. After several trips to hear the teaching they knew they needed to hear it from teachers who spoke their own language.

During this time the chief of the interior began flexing his muscle as leader, and forbade any more listening to the teaching. Tiban would not be stopped. He had heard from the Tadyawan that teachers (the Reeds) were coming who spoke his language. 'We wanted to know if it was good for us to commit ourselves to the new teaching and come to hear you, or if we should stay in the back country. The decision was so important that we killed three chickens for guidance. After we beheaded them we watched. If they flopped towards the interior, then we would stay there. If they flopped towards the lowlands, we would come down to the river to listen.' One chicken flopped towards the back country and two towards the low-lands. Tiban and his people had their answer, and here they were.

The more the Reeds talked with the people, the

more they understood that God's power, rather than God's love, moved a group whose lives were dominated by fear. They began to emphasise Bible stories that demonstrated this power, and they helped the Tawbuid memorise Bible verses to sustain them such as Psalm 56:3—'When I am afraid, I will trust in you.'

Too soon Barbara and Russell had to leave for their furlough in America. Dode and Caroline would be there at the river house for several more months until they too left on furlough. Then the Tawbuid would be on their own. Would they continue to believe the teaching? Or would they go back to their spirit worship, afraid to cross the powerful chief?

'We are to leave all of our old customs that are not good, and do everything that pleases *Funbalugu* even if we have never done it before.' Tiban's words rang in their minds as Russell and Barbara said goodbye to the group and hiked back to the base in Pinamalayan.

Calapan, Mindoro, 1962

Jim Broomhall slipped out of the screen door and found his favourite spot on the wooden bench of the mission home porch. This was the last evening he would sit here watching the sun set over Calapan bay. Jim followed the brilliant blue of a kingfisher flitting from tree to tree and reflected over the past ten years. He had come to Mindoro expecting—expecting what? Expecting to watch God revolutionise the fearsome lives of a trapped people. And he had. Maybe also expecting to be more directly involved with the Mangyan. He loved those survey trips in the old days, tramping through unknown country, feeling like a detective looking for clues to a missing person's whereabouts. Maybe he'd expected to use his medical training more than he had.

He chuckled, remembering the look on Joy Hanselman's face when he ordered her to bed the night he arrived to check on her husband, Bob. From her letter it had sounded like typhoid–and it was. A bad case of typhoid. He remembered the bed sheets hanging from every rafter in that little house. It was hard to dry sheets in the rainy season. 'I'm the nurse tonight,' he'd told her, seeing her exhaustion. It felt good to be able to do something to lighten the load of these men and women who gave so much under difficult conditions.

He noticed how tall the tree had grown in the last year. He'd planted the tropical evergreen when they completed the new mission home. 'These missionaries must have a Christmas tree!' he'd said to Janet. Tonight it made an interesting silhouette against the sky that rapidly turned from red-golds to purple and grey.

Yes, it was good to have had responsibility for this work. To think that there were Mangyan, hundreds of them, who no longer worried about pleasing the capricious spirits, but had confidence in the power and love of God through Jesus Christ–they could celebrate that. With the patient encouragement of the Mindoro team, the Mangyan were beginning to feel (and act) like first-class citizens. They were getting their land registered so it could no longer be stolen from them. Some were learning how to interact with officials and businessmen so they would not be exploited in selling their goods and services. Bringing the tribes together in 'believers' conferences' and offering the short-term Bible schools had helped break down centuries-old walls between tribes. They were learning to work together, something that strengthened their position with the Philippine government.

Neville Cooper had some good ideas about that. Neville, that star of the early Tagalog language studies. He'd do a good job here as Superintendent. Neville was fired up about the Mangyan churches forming an official organisation. It sounded like a good plan. A Christian lawyer from Manila had promised to help. Neville's vision for the Mangyan included a scholarship programme so young people from the tribes could come to secondary school and even college in Calapan. He believed that the Mangyan could get agricultural help from the government, maybe medical and legal aid too.

Well, time will tell. But this would all take much prayer. And there were still tribespeople cowering in the back country who had not been reached. The Reeds had only recently found a large group of Tawbuid in the east. Would they ever find them all? Would the Mangyan believers take responsibility for reaching them? And what about the second generation Mangyan in some tribes whose lives were already being revolutionised by 'civilisation'. Would they remain faithful to the Lord?

It was almost dark. Jim listened to the cockerels crowing in one of the back yards near the road below. There would always be an answering call from another yard. 'The sounds will be the same in Manila,' Jim said to himself, somewhat comforted by the thought. He appreciated this opportunity to now oversee all of the work in the Philippines, and he counted on a good supply of wisdom from the Lord to handle his new assignment.

He rose from the bench and took one more look at the lights twinkling on in the small boats anchored in the bay.

CHAPTER THIRTEEN

I suppose you are wondering why we are building this house when we already have one. But this is not a house. It's what the teachers call a 'church'. It's a place for people to come and hear the new teaching.

You are surprised? Last week my brother went with me to see the teachers. He was still afraid, but he remembered the prophecy of the Old One. You see, these teachers are very much like the prophecy said they would be. And they speak our language.

We stayed with them for two days. Then we asked if they would come here to teach in our village. They will be here in a week's time! My wife has already invited her family to come. I'm sure the shaman will be angry.

There is something about this new teaching that makes me feel safe. I have been afraid for such a long time.

Ayan Bekeg, Mindoro, 1963

Bev Fuller wiped the remains of the sticky rice off three-year-old Jon's face and sent him out to play with three Alangan children who were scrambling up and down a fallen tree trunk. Esther, still a toddler, seemed content to sit on the porch and play with her doll. Bev could hear Daphne MacKenzie, a missionary from Australia, singing while she washed her breakfast dishes in the almost identical Nipa-palm house next door. Already a crowd of children gathered by her steps. They loved to 'test' Daphne on the Alangan words they'd taught her the day before.

Bev heard Jon call to one of the children and thought how quickly he had picked up the language—one of the advantages of living here in this Mangyan village. She glanced out to the porch in time to see Esther reach for a cockroach crawling by her foot. Just one cockroach. How many times they'd slept in a Mangyan house where the thatched ceiling literally crawled with the invincible insects! When roaches got that bad the Mangyan used their own means of pest control. They simply burned the house down and built another. 'Amazing how God changed my mind about raising children in a Mangyan village!' she thought.

She missed Dave. It would be ten more days before he would return from his trip across the island. He'd left a few days ago with Mariano Lakoy, the leader of the Alangan church, and Carding

Bulaklak, the leader of the Iraya church. They planned to hike into the interior and assess what work still needed to be done. The men started out in Iraya country, walking up to the sea and across the rocky northern shore, then down to Abra de Ilog. There they'd check in with two other missionaries, May Roy and Nessie Bell, who would drive them by jeep to the end of the road. Then they'd walk back through Alangan country, finally climbing the back side of Mount Halcon before they returned to Ayan Bekeg. A long trip, but a necessary one if they were to plan for the people and strategy needed in the future.

Maybe she could listen to the morning news before the people started coming. She twisted the knob on their short-wave set. The news programme in progress from DZAS, the Christian station run by Far East Broadcasting Company, came in clearly from Manila. Thank God for the radio. They'd been able to give many of the tribespeople battery-powered radios pre-tuned to DZAS, which now broadcasted a few hours a day in some of the Mangyan languages. 'Portable missionaries' they called these radios.

This morning the news coming from FEBC's Manila studios covered the world—NASA's latest astronaut to orbit the earth twenty-two times, thirty African leaders meet in Addis Ababa to promote African unity, a new programme from the Marcos government. Suddenly Bev stopped breathing. 'From Mindoro,' the newscaster droned, 'a tragic accident yesterday claimed the lives of two OMF missionaries. Information is sketchy, but the accident apparently occurred as they were travelling by jeep to an unknown destination. At least one other person has been injured. More details as they are available.'

'Daphne!' Bev screamed. 'There's been an accident!'

Kasagi, north-western Mindoro, 1963

The bamboo-slat floor creaked with every shift of sixteen Mangyan bodies. For this Sunday service in December, Tibo set the limit at sixteen. 'The others will just have to come later,' he told Hazel. Tibo, one of the Irayas most interested in the message here in Kasagi, had built this house for her. He ought to know how many it could hold.

Hazel hoped that the full house meant open hearts for the message she would bring. Seated in front of the group she could still see over their heads and out of one of the two windows to the clearing where people sat on logs or stood talking, patiently waiting for the 'second service'. Beyond them, a half-hour's walk down the ridge, the lake reflected the morning sun. Ten years ago she'd come to Mindoro hoping to teach as many Mangyan as possible about the God who loved them and wanted to take away their fear. And here she was again back where she started—with the Iraya. This time she'd set a goal to translate the gospel of Mark into the

Western Iraya dialect–significantly different from that of the Eastern Iraya. Of course there was plenty to do besides translation work, but now she had help. She and her new partner would leave soon to visit other inland settlements where they'd not only tell the Christmas story but also gather new words in this western dialect. Right now her partner led the group in a Christmas carol they had translated into Iraya. Hazel usually left the music up to someone else. Singing was not one of her gifts.

A small boy, sitting on his mother's lap, began coughing–a heavy croupy cough. He looked feverish and uncomfortable. The mother patted his back and settled him against her. It seemed to help. Hazel would check on him after the service. She hoped they'd brought in the cholera injections in time. The epidemic further north in Paluan last month encouraged the government to provide vaccine for everyone, including the tribes. Hazel had injected at least sixty Mangyan and treated others for the usual colds, leg sores, and even malaria.

When Hazel read the Christmas story, Tibo nudged his wife. He, like other western interior Irayas, listened with his soul as well as his mind when he heard the message in his own tongue. Many of these people knew no Tagalog–only Iraya. Now that she had returned to them, Hazel was more than ever convinced that these Mangyan must have portions of the Bible in their own language.

Two hours later the people reluctantly left the house, making room for those waiting outside.

Calapan, Mindoro, 1963

By the early 1960s the Christian message had penetrated certain villages in every one of Mindoro's six tribes. But two major challenges faced the missionaries. One was the thousands of Mangyan hidden away in the almost unreachable interior who still had not been contacted. Clearly, many of them would only hear the message if their own tribespeople brought it to them.

The second challenge impacted the first. There were simply not enough missionaries to offer the scattered Christian tribespeople regular teaching to help them grow and be strong in their faith. Every day fledgling Mangyan Christians faced strong temptations to return to the spirit worship of the past.

At the mission home in Calapan one evening in 1963, dinner table conversation turned to the second challenge. Only a dim bulb in the ceiling fixture lit the dining room now that the sun had slipped down into the sea, and every chair was full around the long mahogany table. The meal of chicken livers with rice and vegetables had been served and eaten, but the Mindoro team lingered at the table, continuing the conversation begun early in the day. Bev Fuller reached for a *centores* from the basket in the centre of the table, anticipating the tangy orange flavour of its green fruit, and began to peel it while she listened to the spirited conversation between Dave, Hazel and Frances.

She knew how much Dave wished May Roy were here. May had been enthusiastic about training Mangyan and would have enjoyed this whole day of discussion. They all missed May and Nessie Bell since the accident. Bev remembered her own relief when she heard, from a later radio report, that Dave was not one of the casualties. But she knew his anguish. He couldn't help thinking if only he hadn't accepted the lift to the end of the road, May and Nessie might not have been killed as they drove back to their house. Bless that dear friend in Manila who had advised him, 'Dave, don't second-guess God.'

'The short-term Bible schools we've held in different areas work well to teach the basics,' Dave was saying. 'But if we are to train leaders to take over the work, they will need more than that.' The little Mangyan churches springing up in the tribes couldn't afford to employ a pastor, and no missionary could shepherd all the churches in an area. Besides, every one around the table knew their goal: to work themselves out of a job. Dr B had always reminded them of this. 'We are not the building, nor are we the materials for the building,' he would say. 'We are the scaffolding which only remains until the building can stand on its own.'

'As we said today,' Frances continued the conversation, 'it will be tricky to bring people from different tribes to a central area to live for the length of a Bible-school term. They have different customs, different habits of cooking and eating.'

'I'm concerned about the married men who

would have to leave their wives and children for two to three months at a time,' said Hazel. 'It would be quite a commitment for others to look after their fields.'

Bev wiped the juice from her cheek. 'I agree. That's why it's so important that the Mangyan themselves see the need for this training. How can we help them see this?'

As it turned out, the Mangyan didn't need much convincing. Not long after the discussion in Calapan, Roberto, one of the young men from Ayan Bekeg, told Dave Fuller that he wanted to be a missionary to the Mangyan and would spend three years in Manila in training if that became necessary. Then Jeremias, a Hanunoo from the south, asked for training for the same reason. When the missionaries went to the tribal churches with the idea for a Bible school to train Mangyan leaders, the churches were enthusiastic.

By this time many of the churches collected an offering at their Sunday services. Believers contributed some of the meagre wages they earned from working in a lowlander's fields or selling rattan or bananas. With this money the churches purchased Bibles or helped with expenses of church members travelling to the believers' conferences. As they discussed the proposal for a Bible school, the churches agreed to help support students from their villages who wanted to attend. Other believers would take responsibility for the students' crops for the three months at a time they'd be at the school.

The group at Ayan Bekeg agreed that their village could be the site for the first session. The people there planted more sweet potatoes wherever they found space (they would need extra food) and made plans to build a schoolhouse and a house for Frances Williamson who would teach. Dave and Bev Fuller would oversee the project and assist Frances in teaching.

Two weeks after the first term started, Dave Fuller stood watching some of the students repair his house. 'What a way to begin,' he thought. 'Four typhoons in two weeks!' The typhoon yesterday had blown a wall off the house. He shivered and stamped his feet to get the circulation going. Up here on Mount Halcon the wind and rain could make you quickly forget the sweltering days of the dry season. He wished he had put on a sweater under his rain coat.

Four-year-old Jon ran out from under a neighbour's house where he and some of the other children played. 'Can I help, Daddy?' he asked, pointing to the rain-soaked men tying up the bamboo wall.

'When they have finished, you can help me clean up the mess inside, son,' Dave answered. 'Remember how muddy and dirty everything was when the wind blew the wall down?' Jon ran back under the house, satisfied that his help would be needed.

This had been a real inter-tribal project from the start. Remarkable that the Tadyawan and Tawbuid men had the courage to venture out of their areas and join people from the other tribes in preparing the building that cold wet week before classes began. At first, they wondered if it would work. This was the first time in hundreds of years that people from all the different tribes had worked together and the first time the Tawbuid and Tadyawan had been so far from home. But by the end of the work week, the ice broke and they were singing and praying together with their Christian brothers and sisters.

Classes began the same morning that they said goodbye to the Mangyan who had come to help. Tears still came to Dave's eyes when he realised what God had done. Only a dozen years since the first Mangyan believed, here were sixteen men willing to take three months out of their lives to enrol in the Bible school to become leaders in the Mangyan church. Some had brought their wives and children with them.

He watched their faces that first day as they crouched on the uneven split-log floor of the classroom with no walls, balancing their notebooks on their knees. Some, like Alangan church leader, Mariano Lakoy, peering at the words in his Bible through ill-fitting glasses, looked uncertain, even worried. Others, especially the young ones, seemed ready and eager for the challenge. Jeremias came, grateful to be away from Hanunoo country and the painful memories of the wife he had just lost in childbirth. Roberto had not come. His father, a powerful shaman, forbade him to attend. Dave reminded the group to pray for this young man who must be facing a difficult time right now.

The students were gradually getting used to the timetable—devotions at 7.30 in the morning, followed by four class periods. Afternoons were free for working in the fields, lesson preparation, and remedial reading for those who needed it.

Dave called for Jon as the men finished the wall. Would they have the same diligence to complete the first school term as they were applying to the wall? Some, especially the southerners, weren't used to this cold, and everyone knew they had a limited supply of food. As always, they would trust God for the outcome.

Safa, East Mindoro, 1964

Barbara Reed squinted as her eyes adjusted to the dim light inside the smoky house. Baltugangan, one of the leaders of the thriving Tawbuid church here at Safa, seemed uncomfortable about inviting her in to see the baby born last night. She knew it was two months premature. His wife, Linday, sat by the fire, leaning against the traditional back rest used by Tawbuid women for five days after giving birth. Barbara squatted beside her.

'How is it with you, my friend?' she asked. Linday mumbled and turned away just as Barbara caught sight of the infant. It lay in another corner on a piece of stiff bark, naked and still. The uncut cord and placenta lay beside it. With a feeling of dread, Barbara moved to the corner and touched the little form—a girl, warm and still breathing. A gooey yellow substance had been smeared above the eyes and on her head.

'What's this all over her head?' Barbara asked Linday. She didn't answer. Finally Baltugangan said, 'Sweet potato.'

'What is it for?' she again asked Linday. Neither parent answered.

'But, what's wrong? Why aren't you holding her?'

'It is not our custom,' Baltugangan answered. 'She won't live.' Then he began to explain, but uncertainly, as though unsure about sharing this information. 'This came long before the normal time,' he said, glancing at the newborn baby. 'It is not truly a person. It is just part of the afterbirth. It won't live.'

Barbara felt sick, trying to comprehend the reason for this attitude. It must have something to do with those despicable spirits! Anger rose and tightened her throat as she saw, here in front of her, another example of their insidious power. The Tawbuid were loving parents who cherished their children. But they'd been taught that a premature baby does not live long, and rather than nurture it and then see it die as a real person whose ghost could haunt them, it seemed best to treat it as a non-person in this way.

She didn't know what to say–helpless in the face of this ignorance. The Tawbuid here had been un-usually eager to accept the teaching the Reeds had brought to them. They had continued to meet together and study the few scriptures they had in their language even while the Reeds were on furlough. Now that Russell and Barbara had moved here to live in their village, the Tawbuid had grown in faith at an amazing pace. Some of the men had even walked across the valleys and ridges to help build the new Bible school at Ayan Bekeg. Still, old and destructive customs popped up that needed to be faced. This was one of them.

As gently as she could, Barbara said, 'God wants you to love and care for this tiny one he has given you. Just like he loves you.'

Baltugangan looked at her in surprise. 'Do you mean that . . . God wants us to love this thing?' he stammered. 'Should we hold it–and nurse it?'

'Yes,' she answered, 'and we will help you. Don't worry. I'll be right back.'

Barbara's spirits were lifting as she left and returned in a few minutes with Russell, carrying a cardboard box, soft cloths, and a bottle filled with hot water and covered by a towel. 'Thank you, Lord,' she prayed when she saw that the young couple had cut the birth cord and were now carefully cleaning the sweet potato from the baby's head. She and Russell helped tuck the baby into her new bed next to the warm bottle, and then prayed with Linday and Baltugangan, asking for God's blessing on this family who had the courage to break with the fear-filled customs of the past.

CHAPTER FOURTEEN

It is two dry seasons since the teachers came to us. Every morning we meet in our church to read God's words and pray for the day. We sing too. I'm the leader. The hardest thing for me is the singing. My wife says I sound like a water buffalo with a sore leg! And then she laughs. She does love to laugh, that one.

My brother and I have just returned from the mountain across the valley. We went to help the teachers build houses for the new Bible school. For the first time we saw men and women from some of the tribes to the south and east of us. The first time! We heard that there were such tribes but we had never seen them.

At first we were afraid, but soon we knew that we could be like brothers and sisters because we all have the same Father in heaven. We sang and prayed together and talked about God and Jesus, his son. I will never forget this. The world seems bigger now.

Ayan Bekeg, Mindoro, 1967

The delicious aroma of baking bread filled both rooms of the house. 'It's good to be back.' Bev checked the single loaf in the camping oven. The small metal oven sat on top of a kerosene pressure stove which rested in a five-gallon tin. This protected it from the wind which, even with well-woven grass walls, blew freely enough through the house to extinguish a flame.

She and Dave had taught for three months at a time at each of the different locations of the travelling Bible school. Since the first term of the Mangyan Bible School here in Ayan Bekeg, they made a decision to alternate locations for each term, with one in the south and one in the north. At each place they'd had a dozen or more students, some now close to graduation after attending most of the sessions since the beginning. Most of these students were Mangyan men who wanted to be trained as leaders of the church in their village. Few had any formal education other than literacy classes offered by the missionaries.

'How's that bread coming on?' Dave called out from the other side of the canvas sheet that separated the two rooms. 'It smells wonderful!'

'About fifteen more minutes,' Bev answered. 'But then it has to cool.' She poked her head around the sheet and smiled at the scene. Dave entertained two Mangyan children, as well as four-year-old Esther and two-year-old David, with a large red ball they had purchased in Calapan. Jon, home from his first year at school in Malaysia, played big brother, trying to keep squirming David on his lap.

Bev lifted the oven door for one more quick look at the bread and noticed licks of yellow flame coming out from around the pump area of the stove. That's strange. 'Dave, come and take a look at this, would you?'

Dave came in and checked the flickering flames. Probably, he decided, the safest move would be to carry the whole thing outside. He didn't realise that a tiny hole in the kerosene tank had leaked hot fuel into the bottom of the tin. The resulting fumes ignited into the small flames. When he picked up the tin, the flames connected with the hot kerosene. He took two steps into the next room and the stove exploded into a ball of flame. The children screamed, Bev gasped, and Dave dropped the stove and some-how shoved the five children out of the door to safety. Bev, trapped in the kitchen by what had become a wall of fire, moved quickly to a window and jumped out to the ground. In seconds flames engulfed the grass house.

She found Dave and the children in front of the house. Jon looked terrified and David tried to get his father to pick him up. But she could see that Dave was badly burned. The skin on his face and arms was turning white. 'What should I do?' he asked her, looking at his arms as though they belonged to someone else.

'Run to the river and get in the water,' Bev said as

calmly as she could. She now realised that screams coming from the path were Esther's. She ran to comfort the terrified child and then collected the others who seemed too stunned to move. Mangyan friends came from every direction and gathered outside the burning house. Some of them stayed with the children while she hurried down to the river.

'What will we do? We're eight miles' walk to the nearest transportation into town. Lord, please show us what to do,' she prayed.

'I need to walk for help right now,' Dave said, climbing out of the cool soothing water. 'If I don't I'm afraid I won't be able to make it. I may go into shock. You stay with the children.'

To Bev's relief, Mariano Lakoy ran up just then. 'I'll go with Dave,' he said. 'We'll go as fast as we can. Don't worry.'

Bev watched them start out down the track. It was high noon on one of the hottest days of the year. They had three miles to walk before they could get down the mountain to flat land, and another five miles to the road where they might catch a bus into town. How could they make it in time?

Dave raced down the mountain, lurching around the bends, trying to keep his balance, tripping over stones and roots. The pain was excruciating and he could feel his skin blistering. Half way down he stopped and said to Mariano, 'I'm not sure I can make it. We'd better pray.'

Mariano bowed his head. 'Our Father,' he prayed. 'Dave needs your help. Give him strength to keep going and protect him from the sun. Help us make it to the road and find a way to get to town. Amen.'

At the foot of the mountain Dave got some relief for his scorched skin when he plunged into the river running near the trail. A Mangyan from the village who had followed them down the mountain caught up to them with a sardine can of boiled water for Dave to drink. The next five miles Dave was conscious of only one thing—putting one foot in front of the other.

When they finally reached the road, Dave looked back along the path they'd taken over the flat lands. 'Mariano,' he called. 'Look at that!' With tears of gratitude, Dave pointed at the cloud cover that hung directly over the trail. To the south of the path it rained, and to the north the sun shone brightly. If they'd been in the rain the trail would have been slippery and hard to navigate. If they'd been in the sun his pain would have been unbearable.

Almost before they could absorb this sign of God's care, a petrol truck stopped. Relieved, they climbed on to ride into Calapan.

Meanwhile, up at Ayan Bekeg, the Mangyan fed the children roasted sweet potatoes while Bev looked at the charred remains of the house to see if anything could be salvaged. But they'd lost everything, including Morven Brown's Alangan translation materials. They had been stored in the house waiting for Morven's return, and represented months of work.

A half hour after Dave started out, Bev left the

village with the children and six Mangyan friends. The rain that now fell over the track soaked them all the way down the mountain, making it more of a slide than a walk and temporarily distracted the children from their many questions. Where is Daddy? Is Daddy burned? What about my school-book that got burned up in the house? What about my dolly?

Somehow they found a bus that took them into Calapan and dropped them off at the bottom of the mission home driveway. As soon as they were off the bus, Bev pulled the children along with her as fast as they could go up the steep driveway and burst into the house, frantic to know if Dave had made it. Thank God he had made it and was being treated at the local hospital. More than anything she just wanted to see him.

Later, she sat by Dave's bed in the hospital where a doctor, uneducated in burn therapy, had peeled off the burned skin and swathed him in ointment and bandages. Her whole body sagged in relief, but her insides cringed thinking about his agony. She wished she could take on some of his pain. Her silent prayers for Dave's recovery were interrupted by vivid scenes from the day. The Mangyan bringing them medicines and even money when they saw that all their belongings had been destroyed. The Mangyan taking charge of the children, feeding them, comforting them, going with them down the mountain. Then three Mangyan going with her and the children into town, braving the discrimination of the bus where they were relegated to the back cargo area. She felt proud to sit there in the back with her friends, and maybe even a little amused at the disbelieving stares when Mariano's son put his jacket around wet and shivering Jon. God was giving these Mangyan a new sense of worth and dignity.

After weeks of recovery, Dave seemed well enough to resume his work. The day after he and Bev and the children arrived back in Ayan Bekeg they attended the Sunday worship service. The morning sun reflected off the edge of Mariano Lakoy's glasses as he led the group in a hymn. A lump rose in Dave's throat when he thought of how this man had stuck by him on the day of the fire. Through the window of the church he could see the new house that had been waiting for them when they came up here to Ayan Bekeg yesterday. What a welcome!

All during the painful days in the Calapan hospital, the stressful flight to the hospital north of Manila, and the days of recuperation there, Dave could feel the prayers of the church here in Ayan Bekeg. The crowning moment had come yesterday during a visit to some of the people just after they arrived. Bev told them how thankful she was that Dave got down to the hospital in time. One of the Mangyan said, 'Yes, isn't it wonderful what God does when you missionaries pray?' Dave looked surprised.

'Wait a minute,' he said. 'It was Mariano who prayed for me!'

Their response reminded Dave of the dawn breaking over the sea. God answered the prayer of a

Mangyan for a missionary! They were in this together. They were equal partners. Dave knew he'd remember this moment for ever. 'If this accident has opened their understanding about such an important point, it was worth it all,' he thought.

Bayanan, Mindoro, 1970

Neville Cooper's dream for an association of all the Mangyan churches had become a reality. Each tribe chose a man to represent them on the association's board, and the board had elected officials with specific responsibilities. Yes, the Mangyan church had begun to take shape. Believers from every tribe were filtering God's light into the dark crevasses of fear throughout the mountains of Mindoro. With the purchase of a piece of land on the side of Mount Halcon above Bayanan, the Mangyan now had a permanent site for the Bible school.

During the two-week break between MBS classes, people from three of the six tribes gathered on the Bible school property to learn how to build and teach the first Mangyan Christian Elementary Schools for children. In the past few years on Mindoro, Ann Flory's love and concern for the Mangyan children had pushed her to concentrate much of her effort on their teaching and training. Now she watched a dream come true.

Ann knew this plan would work. She had already tried it with the Hanunoo. Using simple primers written by the missionaries, she had prepared basic material to teach village men, hand-picked by missionaries in each area. Then they taught the children what they had just learned. For tribespeople who were still wary of government schools, this plan could ease children into the education they must have as they faced a future where they would surely be challenged by the outside world.

The first week the men had come to learn how a schoolhouse should look: built level with the ground, not on stilts like their houses, and with windows for good light and one blank wall for the blackboard. Ann had never supervised a building project before, but she had this one all worked out. She knew how large the school should be for each area depending on the number of students. The men watched while Ann showed them how the desks should look: a plank or split bamboo top resting on posts pounded into the ground, and a lower plank or bamboo seat tied to shorter posts to make a seat. Two children would sit at each desk, and the desks in front had to be lower than those at the back so everyone could see the blackboard.

While some of the men went home to build the schools and furniture, Ann began training the ones who would teach. She would supervise the first session in each village. Then the teachers would be on their own. With conflicting emotions Ann prayed as she watched the men leave for their villages after the last training session. She felt as though she'd just taught them to swim for the first time, and then pushed them off the high diving board.

The Bayanan church hosted the ceremonies for the first graduates of the Mangyan Bible School. The day of graduation Frances Williamson and Hazel Page sat across from Mariano Lakoy in the noisy church, full to overflowing with regulars and visitors. Everyone grew quiet as three young men in clean shirts and pressed trousers walked to the front bench and sat down in front of Mariano.

'Mariano must be so proud,' Frances whispered to Hazel. 'Look at the way he's beaming!'

With a prayer, Carding Bulaklak, now the leader of the combined Mangyan churches, opened the ceremonies. Then each of the three graduates stood up and told their story. Jeremias, who started out that first windy, rainy term at Ayan Bekeg shortly after the death of his young wife, told how he had dropped out, discouraged, cold and hungry. 'Then I realised that I must be willing to endure hardship for the Lord,' he said. 'So I returned, and I praise the Lord that I have been able to finish.'

Banya, another Hanunoo tribesman, told about his struggles with finances for school. 'Two years ago I had no money to return to. school. I prayed three times during the night and God reminded me of the place in Hebrews where he says, "I will never leave you or forsake you." That set my mind at rest. I was able to find work and save money to come back to school.' Banya had also helped his father, a shaman, become a believer.

Frances nudged Hazel as Mariano's son, Cesar, stood up. She remembered him coming to classes at the Bible school with his father when he was only twelve. Now Cesar was graduating before his father who had dropped out for a time to work in his fields. But Mariano would graduate too. Frances watched him lean forward and peer through his bifocals. He would not miss a word of what his son said.

'I was only twelve when I invited the Lord Jesus into my heart,' Cesar said. 'My ambition is to teach new believers and bring the good news to others . . . pray for me in the many temptations that come to a young man. I want to follow the Lord faithfully.'

Later, after the diplomas were presented, Frances and Hazel joined Carding Bulaklak and other missionaries and Mangyan church leaders at the front of the church. The three graduates knelt while the others laid their hands on them and committed these young men to God and his plan for them.

'Almost twenty years.' Frances stopped singing for a moment to listen to the voices around her ending the ceremony with the triumphant words of the doxology. How grateful I am for these years—and now it's almost time to leave. Thank you, Lord, for the privilege of seeing this day.

CHAPTER FIFTEEN

Do you remember me? I thought you might have forgotten—it's been such a long time.

Yes, this is my daughter. Isn't she a fine young woman? My wife and I are very proud of her. Especially today. Today she is graduating from the Mangyan Bible School. Not many women have been able to do that. She and her husband have been students there for three years.

You will be surprised when I tell you where they are going. Next week they will travel to another island to live with the Negritos. You may have heard of that tribe. They don't know about God or his Son, Jesus, or any of the stories in the Bible. So my daughter and her husband will tell them.

Yes, it will be difficult for them, but God will take care of them. After all these years, I know that's true. Remember how God found me a good wife and then gave us a healthy baby daughter? Remember how he healed my daughter when she was so sick? And remember how he brought the teachers just like the Old One promised?

Sometimes I think about the prophecy—that the teachers would come. God must have had us on his mind a long, long time ago.

Bayanan, Mindoro, 1971

You could sense the anticipation as the tin-roofed church began to fill with tribespeople from all over Mindoro. There were Hanunoo women from the far south in colourful embroidered blouses and Tawbuid women in soft bark bras. Some Iraya men came in trousers and some Buhid men in loincloths. Many carried cooking pots and extra rice to see them through the days of these meetings. Six years ago at the first Mangyan church conference, no one would have believed that 268 people would fill the chapel today. Ten years ago some of these tribes scarcely knew the others existed.

Today, as another milestone for the Mangyan church, a Christian lawyer from Manila had come with a document which, when signed by the seven Mangyan representatives, would make the Mangyan Tribal Church Association an official corporation under Philippine law. For Neville Cooper, Superintendent of Mindoro, it was another dream come true. The seven men gathered around a wobbly bamboo table, five of them barefoot, and one in a loincloth. The ceremony took over an hour. Perhaps the seven men who signed the document had little idea of the significance of this event, but Neville knew what legal status could mean for the Mangyan churches. They could transact business in the name of the MTCA and they could own property. They could also assist the Mangyan Bible School, now permanently established on property above Bayanan.

Some of those who had gone outside to stretch during the long signing returned and the group began to celebrate the Lord's Supper. Fresh leaves from a tree near the building were passed to each person in the congregation, including the many who overflowed into standing room on each side of the open-walled building. Then leaders passed baskets of broken sweet potato and jugs of water to fill the leaves that served as disposable communion cups.

A Filipino pastor who had befriended the Mangyan gave the talk. 'It is easy to *become* a Christian,' he said, 'but it is hard to *be* a Christian.' This assembly of Mangyan Christians, well acquainted with exploitation and discrimination, knew what he meant. But they knew they were not alone. They had the love and power of the heavenly Father and the encouragement of their brothers and sisters in the other tribes. In spite of their different customs and backgrounds, they could be strong, united in their faith.

North-east Mindoro, 1972

Almost ten years after Hazel Page returned to the Iraya, Mangyan baptised believers on Mindoro

Island numbered between six and seven hundred. The missionaries were primarily there to meet spiritual needs, but now, more than ever, they were faced with the social needs of the Mangyan. In the last ten years the population of Mindoro had doubled, accelerating the push of lowland Filipinos into tribal lands. Unscrupulous land-grabbers sometimes resorted to force if they met resistance from the tribespeople. Missionaries were grateful for the help of Filipino Christian lawyers in legally defending the Mangyan and their lands.

Hazel hoped that the Christian Iraya leader, Tibo, would gain official title to his land at Kasagi in the north-west. Kasagi was one of three villages Hazel now visited regularly, using her translated portions of the New Testament to teach in some of the homes. The progress there and also in Kaagutayan, the Iraya village she visited with Frances Williamson when she first arrived on Mindoro, encouraged her. The Kaagutayan church had been stagnant for a number of years. Then the chapel burned down, and now, in a burst of fresh commitment, the men offered to rebuild it and were collecting one *peso* from each family to purchase a corrugated metal roof.

Would the job ever be finished? After twenty years of work on Mindoro, they were still discovering areas where the people were controlled by fear of demons and had never heard of the power of Jesus Christ. Hazel had been making trips to a village near one of those areas and recently took a group of

Mangyan young adults with her. The story they heard there inspired them all.

They had travelled to this remote village inland from the coast, with enough supplies to stay for at least two weeks of teaching and encouraging. The group of believers, gathered here from three small communities, had grown each time Hazel visited. This time one village had nearly doubled their attendance. What was going on?

The story being told by the Mangyan with the fuzzy, greying beard held the answer. His name was Olohiyo, a believer from this village. 'Early in the summer,' he said, 'when I walked out to San Teodoro on the logging road, I came upon some Tagalog men loading piles of rattan into a truck. The men called to me and ordered me to help them. As a tribesman, of course I had to obey. But that made no difference to the old Iraya who, I discovered later, owned the rattan. When he learned that I had helped the Tagalogs steal the rattan, he threatened to take me to court. I said, "I will do whatever I must to repay your loss."

'"Then you must weed my entire rice field," the old man told me.'

Hazel noticed the young people who had come with her glance at each other. How would they stand such a test, she wondered.

Olohiyo continued his story. 'I went home and prayed with my family about it. Then we all went to the field and began weeding. While we weeded we sang hymns together, and when we sat down to rest we read our Bibles and prayed. My children made friends with the children in the old man's village and taught them songs and Bible verses. It took us three days to weed the field. When we finished, the children of the village begged my youngest daughter to stay longer. On Sunday she brought them to the Christian meeting in our village. Next week they brought others, and soon many people from the old man's village believed, including him.'

Tears filled her eyes as Hazel realised that this was the same old man who had asked them this morning, 'Please, teach me to pray.' Another sign of God honouring the planting of the seed. The seed had taken root! The plant grew. And she had the privilege of watching Iraya Christians discover the power of God's love lived out in the ordinary stuff of life.

Safa, East Mindoro, 1975

Another furlough had come and gone. Another beautiful year with the family all together. It was hard to believe that Becky was engaged and Rick married! Russell and Barbara had been able to attend Rick's wedding just before their return to the Philippines. In Manila they said goodbye to nine-year-old Randy and his little brother, George, off to another school term. As soon as the red mini-bus was out of sight with the seats full of laughing, excited children, Barbara had made her way to a shop where she bought a pair of red and white polka-dot thongs. Funny how a silly thing like that could cheer you up.

Back at Safa with the Eastern Tawbuid, both of them felt their spirits lift when they saw that the believers had grown even more firm in their faith while they'd been away. The tribespeople had taken charge of teaching and preaching, using the Tawbuid Scriptures and other materials which had been translated to this point. One of the Reeds' major tasks would be to finish translating the Bible for these people who spoke almost no Tagalog.

The believers at Safa had developed such a concern for the Tawbuid in the west that they had made several trips with the Reeds to witness to the westerners about their faith. From these trips small groups of believers began to emerge, and now there were three churches in the west. The shamans had great influence in the area, however. They could see themselves losing power as the 'new teaching' took root. More than once they used poison on some groups to give muscle to the ancient hold of the spirits.

After one of those visits to the west, Barbara and Russell sat by the river and watched the water tumble over the huge rocks. In spite of the success of the last trip, Russell could see trouble ahead.

'If these new believers in the west are to keep strong in their faith, someone needs to be there with them–not just visiting them a couple of times a year.'

'But that means either we go and leave the Safa

people without anyone, or we pray and hope for more missionaries,' Barbara reminded him.

'Or someone from each of the three groups there gets enough training to lead them,' said Russell. 'But that could take a long time.'

The Reeds had underestimated the eastern Tawbuid. Before long the elders of each of the three well-established churches met and decided to send a family from their area to live in the west. They would stay for a year, helping the new churches grow. A shy and gentle Tawbuid man offered to go with his family. Then another family volunteered to join the first. Here were twentieth-century Christians with the evangelistic fervour of the first century! What would God do next?

One thing God would do was to watch over his people as land-grabbing in the Safa area became a growing problem. Lowlanders who saw the Mangyan as illiterate and ignorant turned Mangyan fringe areas into fields, and lumber men bulldozed wide ugly roads into the interior in search of prime forest land.

One day eight of these lumber men strode into the Safa chapel and seized it as their headquarters. Not only did they disturb the peace with their loud talking and smoky camp-fires, but they tried to seduce the young girls. The Tawbuid believers, unaccustomed to standing up aggressively for their rights, decided to ask God to handle the situation. They met together and prayed long and seriously, asking God to do something.

A few weeks later, five days of torrential rains brought the whole lumbering operation to a halt, washing deep gullies in their mountain roads. The men eventually left and never returned.

At a feast of thanksgiving, the Tawbuid believers lined up with their banana leaf plates and filled them with fragrant rice. They had much to thank God for this year, but their Christian witness did have opposition. Suklinyan, a Safa church leader who had moved his family to a remote country area to witness to people who were tightly bound by spirit worship, found a spot on the ground beside Barbara and Russell.

'Seven of the leaders in the village where we moved have met and decided the new teaching is not good,' he told them.

'What will you do?' Barbara asked, wondering if this meant another defeat.

'Just keep living there and witnessing,' Suklinyan answered. Barbara sent a silent 'thank you' to the Lord for this courageous man. 'Has anyone told you about the prophecy handed down from our fathers?' Suklinyan asked them.

'Do you mean the one that Tiban's father told him—about the new teaching that would come?'

'Oh, it came many generations before Tiban's father.'

Russell was intrigued. 'Tell us about it.'

'It was handed down from father to son, father to son for many, many years. Our fathers said that white teachers would come and we were to listen and obey their teaching–and we would know who they were because they would know our language.'

Know our language. As far as Russell or Barbara knew, they were the only outsiders who spoke Tawbuid. So that was the reason for the eight years in the west when they felt like failures! All they had done was learn the language!

Back in the west, the Reeds heard another version of the story. 'Our fathers told us that teachers–big people who are white–would come from a far country . . . and they would know our language.'

Suklinyan helped Barbara and Russell trace the prophecy back through sixteen generations–more than three hundred years!

Calapan harbour, Mindoro, 1986

She checked her bags and trunks once more and then dropped into a seat near the port side on the passenger deck of the ferry. Her luggage held precious cargo–Iraya language materials. Hazel might be retiring from the Mindoro field, but she was not retiring from her last major task: to complete a translation of the New Testament for the Irayas in the east. Arlette, the French woman who had been her most recent partner and who was taking her place with the Iraya, was as convinced as Hazel about the need for the translation, and she had a real heart for the interior people. It was good to leave the work with someone like that.

The ferry sailed between the twin islands and

Hazel got up to take one last look at her beloved Mindoro. There, over on the west tucked down in one of the folds between the grey-green mountains. That's where she had spent much of the last thirty-three years—half of her life! How could that many years go by so quickly? To the Lord they were just a blink of his eye. But in that blink he had brought hundreds of Mangyan tribespeople into his family and changed their lives for ever.

Thirty-three years—and before that, China. She couldn't help thinking about China—those brave Christians they had left. Scenes from the last days at the mission compound in Paoshan played through her mind. 'Did anyone find my Handy Andy under the steps,' she wondered.

Mindoro faded from view, blocked by the hulk of Verde Island, and Hazel felt a sadness slip over her. So many memories, so many dear friends—some of them, like Anghel Anias, already home with the Lord. She could almost smell Anghel's talcum powder as she pictured him there on their tiny porch in Kaagutayan. Surely God had prepared that man to be their first language helper. And Palay, that curly-haired boy, now a grown man with a family, still tramping the hills in search of someone who may not have heard the good news.

A small boat pulled out of a dock off Verde's east side. 'Probably going fishing,' she pondered. 'Fishing. That's the kind of thing you're supposed to do when you retire. Relax and take it easy and go fishing. I certainly don't feel ready for retirement. I'll just get that translation done and surely the Lord will have something else for me.' She wondered what Frances thought about retirement. She'd been at it for ten years, now. Before she left, Frances had been able to see Mariano graduate from the Mangyan Bible School. That was quite a year. Not only Mariano, but the first woman graduated in that class.

Things were changing, no doubt about that. How would the children of the first generation of believers, some of them with families of their own, handle the way their world was shifting? As life improved economically, it became more complicated, with greater needs. These young people had a set of challenges their parents had never dreamed of, and many of them could not imagine a life where 'spirits' controlled the days and nights.

Hazel sighed. 'Each generation has its own challenges and opportunities. But God never changes.' She dropped back into her seat. What were the words to that familiar old hymn—the one the missionaries sang so often when they'd get together? And then she could almost hear the group—the way they sounded in the early years, singing in harmony, without instruments: 'Tis Jesus, the first and the last, whose Spirit shall guide us safe home. We will praise him for all that is past, and trust him for all that's to come.'

Shanghai, China, 1991

Hazel glanced out of the window by her desk and saw the last light wink off in the eight-storey office building across the yard. She really should heat up some soup. That's all she wanted: soup and her special 'tea'—hot water with milk—and maybe some of those rusks they sent over from the kitchen with a little strawberry jam.

They took good care of her here. When the Shanghai Boiler Works asked her to come and teach English to their employees, they offered her this large room with kitchenette and bath right on the company's multi-acre complex. Daisy, the pretty young Chinese woman in charge of foreign visitors for the company, had become a friend who graciously looked after Hazel's needs.

It was another one of the Lord's surprises to be back in China. A different China, to be sure. But the people were the same. Then there was the award. Such a surprise! Daisy had come with the news today, and seemed to think it was very important. Earlier in the year the Shanghai Boiler Works had nominated Hazel for the prestigious Magnolia award given each year to a foreigner who had made special contributions to the city of Shanghai. And she had won!

'I wonder what the Lord has in mind to have worked out something like this? As always, you know my desire is that my life will honour you. Now, Lord, may you be honoured through this award.'

She peered over her bifocals to switch on the shortwave radio—a little bit of news to accompany her meal. Then she got up and put the kettle on the hot plate in the hall. She'd just have a light supper and then turn in early. It had been a busy day.

APPENDIX 1

AFTERWORD

The story of God's work in the hearts of the Mangyan of Mindoro is not finished. Nor has the work been accomplished only through the people who are named in this book. Many people–some living and some who have gone on–played as large or larger a role than those who have been included. But all, whether in the book or not, would agree that they were simply part of God's plan to reach one more group of people with the good news of salvation through Jesus Christ.

But what about the Mangyan church of the 1990s? Have all of the Mangyan of Mindoro, now estimated at fifty or sixty thousand, been reached with the gospel?

As with a church body anywhere else in the world, the state of the Mangyan church today is both encouraging and discouraging. Adjusting from the stone age to the twentieth century within one generation has had a devastating effect on some tribespeople. The missionaries see the confusion of Mangyan whose children have been born into a materialistic culture the parents are not yet used to. Mangyan church leaders face the temptation of succumbing to the pressures of government parties who want to use their influence. Believers are sometimes confused by the many religious groups now pouring into Mindoro with their own twist on the gospel message. Old animistic beliefs die hard, and some believers still find it difficult to give up spirit practices. Strong Mangyan clans can cause factionalism in churches, and young leadership must yield to old, even when the older is not leading with wisdom and grace.

Even so, the goals first spelled out by Dr Jim Broomhall in the early 1950s are being realised. The tribal church is in capable Mangyan hands and, though missionaries continue to advise and encourage, only a few places have OMF missionaries in residence. Each tribe has Scripture in their own language. The Iraya New Testament was completed in 1991 before Hazel Page left for China to teach English at the Shanghai Boiler Works. Never content to sit and watch the world go by, Hazel returned to Mindoro for a few months in 1995 to help Arlette Dombre finish a new Iraya dictionary.

Elly van der Linden completed a Hanunoo New Testament before she retired to the Netherlands. Before Caroline Stickley left Mindoro to care for her ailing mother, she and Dode Pack translated sections of the New Testament into Tadyawan.

Morven Brown completed an Alangan translation, and Bob and Joy Hanselman finished the Buhid New Testament before their retirement. Barbara and Russell Reed, who left Mindoro in 1994, spent the first months of their retirement putting the finishing touches on the Tawbuid New Testament.

Armed with God's word in their own tongue, Mangyan believers have taken responsibility for penetrating the hidden valleys and almost inaccessible mountain areas where unreached Mangyan still hide. Insurgent activity has made it more difficult to travel and live in certain places and has even threatened the lives and property of both Mangyan and missionaries.

The Mangyan Bible School, still clinging to the craggy side of Mount Halcon, is directed and taught by Mangyan. OMF missionaries serve in an advisory capacity. For years Ninardo was a much-loved member of the MBS faculty. Now arthritis, which in his last year of teaching forced him to a painful crawl up to the classroom, has ended his teaching days. Bado, one of the school's first graduates and its first Mangyan director, continues to help MBS with business matters.

The effect of Mangyan lives changed by the grace of God through Christ has been felt beyond Mindoro. In 1979 Mangyan believers became concerned for the Negritos on a neighbouring island. Roberto (the young Alangan whose shaman father kept him from attending the first MBS classes) and Jeremias (the Hanunoo from the first MBS class) visited the island with one of the missionaries. At the next intertribal believers' conference, Jeremias and Roberto told about finding frightened, underfed Negrito slave workers who asked them, 'Does your coming mean life or death for us?' Mangyan believers were touched by the plight of these neighbours, partly because of their own struggle with exploitation and fear. They began raising money to send Mangyan missionaries to the Negritos. Jeremias was one of the first to go.

Bev and Dave Fuller left the Mangyan Bible School in 1975 to go to the island of Mindanao, south of Mindoro, where OMF had begun a new work among the Manobo tribe. One of the highlights of their six years there was a visit by a group of quiet Mangyan Christians who inspired the fierce spear-carrying Manobo to follow the Mangyan practice of worshipping together every evening after work is done. Bev and Dave returned to Mindoro to direct the OMF language school where all new missionaries now study Tagalog before going out into their designated areas. In 1995 Dave and Bev Fuller retired to Canada.

Frances Williamson, Dr Jim Broomhall and Hanni Kaspar have joined Marie Barham, May Roy and Nessie Bell in heaven.

Overseeing the work of OMF on Mindoro has never been an easy job. Jim Broomhall sensed keenly his dependence on God's wisdom for the job, as did those who succeeded him. To strike a balance between the Filipino work in the lowlands (that began when early missionaries kept their base homes there) and the work with the tribes is a continuing challenge.

Anni Bosch, a Swiss woman who worked with the Alangan for many years, has been instrumental in maintaining a focus on the tribal work in her role as Mangyan Ministries Coordinator.

With the untiring help of Christian Filipino lawyers, the solid organisation of Mangyan churches has built programmes to educate young people through a scholarship plan and dormitory in Calapan. They have encouraged new crop methods and money-making efforts for the villages, and have helped certain tribespeople have a voice in government.

Years ago, God prepared the Mangyan people to receive the new teaching and then prepared missionaries to carry it to them. Here on Mindoro there is a confidence that what God has begun, God will complete.

APPENDIX 2

FROM A MANGYAN CHRISTIAN LEADER

'In your oneness with him, you have grown in all ways, both in word and in knowledge. The truth we preached about Christ is clearly seen in you' 1 Corinthians 1:5–6 (literal translation).

This truth is evident in our lives. Before the good news came to us we couldn't read or write, schools were far away and we were afraid of anybody we didn't know, especially if they wore clothes! We wore only loincloths and weren't used to clothes or sandals. We practised slash-and-burn farming, ate bananas, yams and some rice. I couldn't attend public school but was taught to read and write by missionaries. When we received the good news, a great change occurred in our lives and situation.

In 1968 the Mangyan Bible School started and relationships between Mangyan groups began to develop and, little by little, even with non-tribal people of Mindoro. Our minds were opened and we saw the importance of studying. Today many

Mangyan have completed studies while others are still in school. Mangyan are now established to teach the word of God.

Back then, Mangyan weren't ready to leave home for fear of the spirit of darkness. Now some have moved to the other side of Mindoro, to Camarines Sur and Palawan, as missionaries. We are now open to irrigation instead of slash-and-burn farming. Before, we needed only pigs for meat but now we use water buffalo or even small tractors for making fields. When Mangyan used to talk with others they wouldn't look them in the face because they were shy, but now they are able to talk straightforwardly with anyone.

All of this is the result of God's work through the good news that was preached to us. There is still the challenge of many more Mangyan to be reached and their lives changed in Christ. May God use OMF throughout the world to bring many more into the kingdom of God.

Sano Pablo
President, Mangyan Tribal Church Association

APPENDIX 3

OMF MISSIONARIES WORKING WITH THE MANGYAN*

Frances Williamson (USA), 1952–1973, Iraya and Mangyan Bible School

Dr Jim and Janet Broomhall (UK), 1952–1961, Superintendent

Hazel Page (Canada) 1953–1986, Iraya, Alangan, Hanunoo

Bob and Joy Hanselman (USA, Australia), 1953–1989

Russell and Barbara Reed (USA), 1953–1994, Tawbuid

Caroline Stickley (USA), 1953–1979, Iraya and Tadyawan

* Dates shown are the years of Mangyan ministry only; many missionaries have worked with other groups either before or afterwards. Where a husband and wife started their Mangyan ministry in different years, we have taken the earlier year in each case.

This list also includes people whose ministry has supported the Mangyan church indirectly. It is always difficult to draw up a comprehensive list, and we apologise for any names we have omitted.

Cyril and Doris Weller (Canada), 1953–1965,
Superintendent
Marie Barham (Canada), 1954–1957, Iraya and
Buhid
May Roy (New Zealand), 1954–1963, Iraya
Dr Colin and Gertrude Tweddell (Australia/
USA), 1954–1963, Iraya
Margrit Furrer (Switzerland), 1954–1959,
Iraya
Betty Paeth (USA), 1954–1958, Iraya
Shirley Jean Wing (USA), 1954–1961, Iraya
Morven Cree Brown (New Zealand), 1954–1989,
Alangan
Mary Jane Thompson Dick (USA), 1954–1971,
Tadyawan
Fay Goddard (USA), 1955–1960, Buhid
Darlene Anthens (USA), 1955–1958, Iraya
John and Juanita Thompson (USA), 1955–1956,
Iraya
Dorothy Reiber (USA), 1955–1980, Buhid
Betty Jean Nichols (USA), 1955–1959, Iraya
Neville and Joan Cooper (Australia), 1956–1976,
Buhid
Ellie van der Linden (Netherlands), 1956–1992,
Hanunoo and Mangyan Bible School
David and Beverley Fuller (Canada/USA),
1956–1974, Alangan
Tom and Caroline Graumann (UK/USA),
1957–1966, Iraya, Mangyan Bible School
Niklaus and Doreen Wehren (Switzerland/UK),
1957–1961, Hanunoo

Daphne McKenzie (Netherlands), 1958–1968,
Alangan

Ann Flory (USA), 1958–1986, Hanunoo and
Schools

Werner and Doris Demand (Switzerland),
1958–1996, Iraya, Mangyan Bible School

Doris Pack (Canada), 1959–1978, Tadyawan

Daphne Parker (UK), 1959–1963, Iraya

Nessie Bell (UK), 1961–1963, Iraya

Andreas and Ruth Fahrni (Switzerland),
1962–1991, Mangyan Bible School,
Superintendent

Nick and Ivy Gawryletz (Canada), 1959–1971,
Buhid

Shirley Charlton (South Africa), 1963–1979,
Iraya

Karl and Waltraut Lagerhausen (Germany/
Switzerland), 1962–1972, Hanunoo

Theo and Maria Herren (Switzerland), .
1964–1986, Iraya, Superintendent

Hanni Kaspar (Switzerland), 1965–1997,
Tadyawan, Mangyan Bible School

Jean Govan (UK), 1965–1981, Tadyawan,
Mangyan Bible School

Gwen Lay (New Zealand), 1965–1966, Hanunoo,
Mangyan Bible School

Hermann and Doris Elsaesser (Germany),
1967–1985, Iraya, Mangyan Bible School

✗**Anni Bosch** (Switzerland), 1971–present, Alangan,
Mangyan Ministries Co-ordinator

Ingeborg Linder (Germany), 1971–1984, Iraya

Larry and Anita Dubois (USA), 1974–1981,
Tawbuid

Gillian Hunt (UK), 1975–1984, Iraya

William and Marlene Doust (Australia),
1976–1984, Tawbuid

Hans-Hermann and Erika Heldberg (Germany),
1978–1997, Alangan, Superintendent

Dr Don and Penny Enarson (Canada/USA),
1979–1980, Mangyan medical

Frances Bezemer (Netherlands), 1980–1989,
Hanunoo

Arlette Dombre (Switzerland), 1981–present, Iraya
and translation

Jean van der Flier (Netherlands), 1982–1985, Iraya

Tom and Vicki Tweddell (USA), 1985–1990,
Mangyan radio

Tobias Appius (Switzerland), 1988–1990,
Mangyan agriculture

Spring Lai (Hong Kong, SAR), 1988–1992, Iraya

Derek and Liz Daniel (UK), 1989–present,
Tawbuid translation

Martin and Alexandra Haworth (UK),
1994–present, Buhid

Ernst and Sonja Diggelmann (Switzerland),
1995–1997, Superintendent

Anne Bruning (New Zealand), 1996–present,
Mangyan Bible School

John and Paula Richards (UK), 1997–present,
Mindoro Regional Director

APPENDIX 4

BOOKS

OMF International works in East Asia, and among East Asian peoples around the world. It was founded by James Hudson Taylor in 1865 as the China Inland Mission. The overall purpose of its ministry, including its book publishing, is to glorify God through the urgent evangelisation of East Asia's millions.

OMF publishes titles to motivate Christians for world mission, and to equip them for playing a part in it. These include:

- stories and biographies related to God's work in East Asia
- accounts of the growth and development of the Church in Asia
- contemporary mission issues
- the biblical basis of mission
- studies of Asian culture and religion relating to the spiritual need of her peoples

English speaking OMF centres

Australia: PO Box 849, Epping, NSW 2121

Canada: 5759 Coopers Ave, Mississauga ON L4Z 1R9

Malaysia: 3A Jalan Nipah, off Jalan Ampang, 55000 Kuala Lumpur

New Zealand: PO Box 10–159, Auckland, 1030

Philippines: PO Box 1997–1159, QCCPO, 1100 Quezon City

Singapore: 2 Cluny Road, Singapore 259570

South Africa: PO Box 3080, Pinegowrie 2123

UK: Station Approach, Borough Green, Sevenoaks, Kent TN15 8BG

USA: 10 West Dry Creek Circle, Littleton, CO 80120–4413

Also distributed in the Philippines by: OMF Lit. 776 Boni Avenue, Mandaluyong City, Metro Manila. This title is published by OMF International (UK). Visit our website at *www.omf.org.uk*